WHAT YOUR COLLEAGUES ARE SAYING . . .

A must-read for classroom teachers, for teacher leaders/mentors, for teachers—in-training, and for teachers' instructors. All great teachers know that there are five essential things that they need to know and do to create a dynamic classroom. This book answers the five "big questions." In our current environment, teachers are asking for help creating a dynamic classroom. There isn't another book on the market like it. This book is the answer to how to create a dynamic classroom that is student-centered, engaging, relationship-building, goal-oriented, and lively.

—Edward DeRoche
Director, Character Education Resource Center
Department of Learning & Teaching, University of San Diego

Serena Pariser and Victoria Lentfer offer us exemplary classroom practices, teacher wisdom, and a healthy dose of optimism. They encourage us to "take a deep breath" and intentionally choose our next small step. The answers in this book can minimize stress, help teachers avoid burnout, and improve teacher retention.

—Carol Pelletier Radford
Author of *Teaching With Light*, *Mentoring in Action*, and *The First Years Matter*

Serena Pariser and Victoria Lentfer's *Answers to Your Biggest Questions About Creating a Dynamic Classroom* provides newer teachers with answers to common questions that linger in the brain of a newer teacher. As a newer teacher myself, I wish a book like this existed when I started out. This book is engaging, informative, and so much more. If you know a new teacher, work with a new teacher, or are a new teacher, this book is absolutely for you and will make the perfect gift for a new teacher in your life. Each section includes helpful tips and is easily organized and accessible. This book is truly an amazing guide for newer teachers, and I highly recommend it as it will form the perfect basis for that exciting and powerful start of a new journey. Teaching can be many things, but this book is truly a game changer for anyone starting out.

—Susan Jachymiak
Teacher, Leader, and Author

Answers to Your Biggest Questions About Creating a Dynamic Classroom embraces the need for engagement of both the student and the teacher. It's a book that not only helps a student to thrive as a learner but also helps a teacher to thrive as a coach, a guide, and a facilitator. Each chapter launches with an "Imagine This" scenario, and then breaks down and deconstructs what makes that moment in the classroom engaging and successful. The suggestions nod to what we all feel in the moment of classroom stress and give alternate solutions that are efficient and doable. This is a book that shares strategies for Monday, not someday.

—Heather Wolpert-Gawron
(aka "tweenteacher")
Author of *Just Ask Us: Kids Speak Out on Student Engagement*

ANSWERS *to Your*

BIGGEST QUESTIONS *About*

CREATING A DYNAMIC CLASSROOM

This book is dedicated to those who have chosen to enter this beautiful profession.
May your journey be one filled with immense gratitude.

FIVE to THRIVE

ANSWERS *to Your* BIGGEST QUESTIONS *About*

CREATING A DYNAMIC CLASSROOM

Serena Pariser
Victoria Lentfer

For information:

Corwin
A SAGE Company
2455 Teller Road
Thousand Oaks, California 91320
(800) 233-9936
www.corwin.com

SAGE Publications Ltd.
1 Oliver's Yard
55 City Road
London, EC1Y 1SP
United Kingdom

SAGE Publications India Pvt. Ltd.
B 1/I 1 Mohan Cooperative
Industrial Area
Mathura Road, New Delhi 110 044
India

SAGE Publications
Asia-Pacific Pte. Ltd.
18 Cross Street #10–10/11/12
China Square Central
Singapore 048423

President: Mike Soules
Vice President and Editorial
  Director: Monica Eckman
Executive Editor: Tori Mello Bachman
Content Development
  Editor: Sharon Wu
Editorial Assistant: Nancy Chung
Production Editor: Tori Mirsadjadi
Copy Editor: Meg Speer-Levi
Typesetter: Integra
Proofreader: Lawrence W. Baker
Indexer: Maria Sosnowski
Cover Designer: Gail Buschman
Marketing Manager:
  Margaret O'Connor

Printed in Canada

Library of Congress Cataloging-in-Publication Data

Names: Pariser, Serena, author. | Lentfer, Victoria, author.
Title: Answers to your biggest questions about creating a dynamic classroom :
  five to thrive / by Serena Pariser and Victoria Lentfer.
Description: Thousand Oaks, California : Corwin, 2023. | Series: Corwin
  teaching essentials
Identifiers: LCCN 2022001201 (print) | LCCN 2022001202 (ebook) |
  ISBN 9781071856789 (paperback) | ISBN 9781071880708 (adobe pdf) |
  ISBN 9781071880692 (epub) | ISBN 9781071880685 (epub)
Subjects: LCSH: Classroom management. | Classroom environment.
Classification: LCC LB3013 .P279 2023 (print) | LCC LB3013 (ebook) |
  DDC 371.102/4--dc23/eng/20220315
LC record available at https://lccn.loc.gov/2022001201
LC ebook record available at https://lccn.loc.gov/2022001202

This book is printed on acid-free paper.

22 23 24 25 26 10 9 8 7 6 5 4 3 2 1

DISCLAIMER: This book may direct you to access third-party content via web links, QR codes, or other scannable technologies, which are provided for your reference by the author(s). Corwin makes no guarantee that such third-party content will be available for your use and encourages you to review the terms and conditions of such third-party content. Corwin takes no responsibility and assumes no liability for your use of any third-party content, nor does Corwin approve, sponsor, endorse, verify, or certify such third-party content.

Note From the Publisher: The authors have provided video and web content throughout the book that is available to you through QR (quick response) codes. To read a QR code, you must have a smartphone or tablet with a camera. We recommend that you download a QR code reader app that is made specifically for your phone or tablet brand.

CONTENTS

ACKNOWLEDGMENTS

[Serena]

A teacher's journey contains many people and lessons along the way. I'd like to acknowledge those who helped my journey and sincerely express my gratitude.

My first sixth-grade math class in West Philadelphia, which taught me you must connect with students before and during teaching content. Thank you for also showing me what happens when you do not!

Gompers Preparatory Academy and Vincent Riveroll for showing me what it truly means to connect with a child.

Dr. Orletta Nguyen for showing me, among many things, how to make curriculum that can transform a student's life.

Linda Mello for working with me as a co-teacher, through thick and thin, and helping us become the dynamic duo for students.

Dr. Victoria Lentfer for your partnership and dynamic work with teachers.

My former graduate students at the University of San Diego, who shed light on the experiences of newer teachers in today's world.

The University of San Diego for giving me opportunities to see the bird's-eye view of the bigger picture in the world of education.

My aunt, Carla Pariser, for always being willing to share insight on topics that relate to any field of work, including work/life balance.

My family and Dad and Mel for always being supportive during the book writing process.

Dr. Edward DeRoche for introducing me to the book publishing world and starting so many sentences to me with "In your next book. . . ."

Corwin for being supportive, always.

And finally, I'd like to express endless gratitude to Tori Mello Bachman, editor at Corwin, for going above and beyond and bringing this book to life.

[Vicki]

I want to thank my family and friends for their love and support, and all of my students for their insights and for challenging me to be a better teacher and person.

I want to thank Serena Pariser for her work and dedication to this book; her expertise and passion shine throughout this book and her work.

PUBLISHER'S ACKNOWLEDGMENTS

Corwin gratefully acknowledges the contributions of the following reviewers:

Nicholas Pyzik
Elementary Mathematics Resource Teacher
Baltimore County Public Schools

Crystal Wash
Executive Director, Consortium for Educational Research and Advancement
Chicago, IL

ABOUT THE AUTHORS

 **Serena Pariser** is the best-selling author of *Real Talk About Classroom Management* and *Real Talk About Time Management*. She taught for many years as an English teacher, mostly in San Diego and one year in Philadelphia. She has experience working in some of the most challenging school settings from coast to coast. In addition to her extensive experience in urban school settings, she also has experience in affluent schools and has truly seen all sides of education. Serena was humbled to be recognized as Teacher of the Year at Gompers Preparatory Academy.

Her passions include progressive classroom management best practices, bringing curriculum to life, time management for teachers, and weaving character education into the curriculum. She presents on these topics at educational conferences around the country. She was a keynote speaker for the Arizona K12 Center Beginning Teacher Institute Conference, the Illinois New Teacher Collaborative Beginning Teacher Conference, and the Alabama-Mississippi Teachers of English to Speakers of Other Languages Conference.

She worked as assistant director of Field Experience at the University of San Diego, where she has a broader influence on new teachers entering the profession. In addition, Serena was selected to be a National Evaluator for Schools of Character.

In addition to her educational work in the United States, Serena has expanded her educational knowledge around the globe. She coached teachers and modeled best practices and engagement strategies in Kathmandu, Nepal. Serena was selected as a U.S. ambassador with the Fulbright Distinguished Awards in Teaching Program, which gave her an opportunity to coach teachers in the village of Molepolole in Botswana.

Serena has an international audience of educators on social media, all found on her website at www.serenapariser.com, where she writes educational articles for teachers.

 **Dr. Victoria Lentfer** is author of the best-selling book *Keep Calm and Teach: Empowering K–12 Students With Positive Classroom Management Routines*. Her book has been highly praised by Dr. Susan Swearer from the University of Nebraska-Lincoln. Dr. Swearer is the chair of the Research Advisory Board for Lady Gaga's Born This Way Foundation. Dr. Lentfer is a personal life coach, an educational consultant, and founder of the CALM Classroom Management Program, which is a comprehensive behavior management and teacher leader program that provides communication models to guide teachers and students to an inclusive and productive classroom. Dr. Lentfer offers professional learning for new teachers and veteran teachers in the area of classroom management. She has recently founded the Summer Seminar Courses in Classroom Management and Personal Growth for Teachers. She has more than 20 years of experience providing instructional support and teaching in urban, suburban, and rural districts, and has done extensive work with incarcerated youth. She is an education lecturer at the University of Nebraska Omaha, where she teaches classroom management and middle-level courses. Visit Dr. Lentfer's website at https://www.victorialentfer.com for more resources and opportunities to connect.

Imagine your class of 33 students entering the classroom. They immediately know where to get their notebooks and other materials for class. They sit down without disrupting their peers and begin to work on their question prompt. They know this is the beginning-of-class routine and do it seamlessly without any verbal reminder from you. They know how to do this because they have had an opportunity to practice it and you have consistently done it every day since the first week of school.

The bell rings; you come in from monitoring the hallway between classes and observe all your students focused on their work. You proceed to take attendance, then talk with Sam regarding his missing assignments, all while students are quietly working on the question prompt you posted at the front of the classroom. The co-teacher in your classroom walks around the room and checks for completion of last night's homework. The classroom vibe is happy; students feel relaxed, comfortable, and valued. It's a place both you and your students want to be every day.

You begin the lesson with an anticipatory set that captures students' attention, a quick, five-minute introduction to the lesson topic. It engages the students with an interactive role-play, images, and possibly manipulatives to consider—not to answer questions but to lead them into thinking about the concepts. This helps students start to predict what may be around the corner for the lesson. It leaves them with a grand sense of anticipation because they hang on the edge of their seats with more questions than answers. It leads them with curiosity and prepares them for a journey of discovery.

You have captured your students, and now they are focused and want to learn; so you dive into the lesson. You teach a 10- to 20-minute whole-group lesson, and the students are practicing the concept afterward collaboratively. Your students work really well together, and you have done extensive work behind the scenes to teach this skill. You then indicate the behavior expectations for partner work. They follow your instructions. There's a sense of mutual respect between you and your students. Students raise their hands when they need to answer or ask a question. You observe your students helping other students during partner and small-group work. Students use appropriate voice levels. You finish the lesson by having the students complete an exit ticket to show they understood the material. The bell rings, and the students file out of the classroom as you tell them thank you and wish them a wonderful day. They wish you the same.

Your students know you post their assignment on the left-hand side of the board. Your students can also turn in their work and put away their materials in an efficient and orderly fashion. Your students do not feel pressured not to make a mistake, because you have established a safe and inclusive classroom. They know they are welcome because they can see themselves represented on the walls. Your students know they can engage in conversations in a respectful manner.

All your students feel safe and supported. Your classroom is dynamic.

Imagine this as your reality.

What are the biggest questions teachers ask about creating a dynamic classroom? The five main questions that title the five chapters in this book will serve as a guiding framework for creating a dynamic classroom:

1 How Do I Build an Affirming Classroom Community?
2 How Do I Keep Students at the Center?
3 How Can I Design Effective, Fun, and Engaging Learning for Students?
4 How Can I Make Assessments Work for Me and My Students?
5 What Are the Things I Need to Know . . . But Are Rarely Discussed in a Teacher Training Program?

Often we overlook what actually makes the fabric of a dynamic classroom and spend our days "getting by and settling for a classroom that is just good enough." The majority of teachers report loving their job. Let's hold on to that—even on days when you're not feeling your most dynamic self. (And if you are in the 4 percent who don't love your job, let's see if we can get you back to the other side.) Let this book be your coach, shoulder, and safety net. We're here to dissect the five most critical things you can address to have this type of classroom and overall more happiness every day doing what you love to do. Let us get you on the right foot, or maybe get *back* on the right foot. The advice in this book is research based and tried and true in the experiences of teachers. You and your students deserve to be thriving instead of surviving.

Each chapter provides practical guidance on what you need to succeed, answering sub-questions about things like building routines, providing equitable classroom management, planning lessons that allow for differentiation, using technology effectively, minimizing off-task behaviors, and much more. And the final chapter covers important areas that are often overlooked in teacher prep programs but can make or break a teacher in their early career, such as communicating with parents, asking for administrator support, and maintaining a healthy work/life balance.

WHAT IS A DYNAMIC CLASSROOM?

By this, in the simplest form, we mean that your classroom is a place of positivity, and more importantly, it is full of energy. This energy could look like students almost jumping out of their seats to answer a question during a debate, or it could look like students focusing intensely on writing a personal narrative that creatively expresses an important moment in their life. It could also look like students in a group having a heated discussion on whether George made the right decision for Lenny at the end of Steinbeck's *Of Mice and Men*.

Regardless of how this energy looks, it is in a form that is the opposite of apathy or disengagement. Yes, your dynamic classroom might be a bit louder than your neighbor's classroom sometimes, but that's because your students are excited to learn! In your dynamic classroom, learning is a social activity. Students can work together without conflict, they feel emotionally supported to share ideas and challenge each other, and there's a constant buzz of excitement and energy in the air during the lessons. A dynamic classroom is affirming and puts students, instead of just the curriculum, in the center. This type of classroom brings student voice into the lessons, and brings effective, fun, and engaging learning to students. A dynamic classroom has well-planned curriculum that constantly assesses student learning in creative and effective ways. In a dynamic classroom, the teacher fosters relationships with the students and they know their teacher cares about them both as human beings and as students.

WHO IS THIS BOOK INTENDED FOR?

If you are a new teacher, this book will set you up for success in the first few years, when habits are formed. It's really tough to unlearn bad teaching habits, and most of us are guilty of forming at least one or two bad habits the first few years. Serena recalls, for example, in her second year of teaching, a parent was so upset about her daughter's low grade in English class that the student's mother, aunt, and friend all came directly to her door while she was in the middle of teaching a class. Serena's entire class had to watch her get "told off" by these three adults. Serena feels that if she'd had the answers that are in this book then, she would have known how to diffuse an angry parent *and* how to collaborate with them to support the student together. She also would have known to reach out earlier and what to say to the parent before the situation escalated to such heated emotion. This is just one example of how this book can help new teachers.

If you are an experienced teacher who wants support to create and sustain a more dynamic classroom, the strategies in this book can get you there. Serena was lucky enough to work with a mentor, who also happened to be her co-teacher, who helped shape her from that teacher who was pretty good to a teacher who had a dynamic classroom full of students excited and eager to learn. Just one example of this is in Chapter 3, where highly engaging, fun, and collaborative learning strategies other than direct instruction are explained. Including these types of strategies in Serena's lessons often was just one factor that had her students asking, "How do you make teaching so fun, Ms. Pariser? We feel so happy while we are learning."

If you are a mentor teacher, teacher leader, or teacher coach, this book can help support you in leading newer teachers or teachers who need a little extra support to create classrooms that are dynamic and where learning is brought to life. Serena used to coach teachers and worked with a high school biology teacher who had a strong mastery of science content but lacked the ability to form relationships with his students because so many off-task behaviors were happening during the lesson. In turn, the students didn't appreciate his content mastery. It was a lose-lose situation. The information in this book can help support teachers like this, who have student-centered goals but aren't sure how to achieve them. Perhaps, as a teacher leader, you can use this book to support those teachers you are coaching, leading, and mentoring. For example, in Chapter 2 you'll find creative and effective ways teachers can efficiently build relationships with their students with very little time or effort.

The teachers whom you work with also can learn that teachers who report having strong relationships with their students report having 31 percent fewer behavioral issues (Marzano et al., 2003).

If you are a teacher educator, this book is a visually appealing and engaging text that can support preservice teachers in starting on the right foot. It can set them up for success in being the teacher and having the classroom that so many visualize when they enter education programs. For example, in Chapter 5, readers will learn myriad solutions to issues that may arise that we don't learn about in teacher prep programs. For example, teacher prep programs rarely guide us on how to navigate a difficult parent meeting; this is often an in-the-moment lesson learned through trial and error, which can take an emotional toll on a teacher. Chapter 5, in just a few pages, offers guidance and resources to help with parent communication and so much more. How much better will our teachers of tomorrow be set up for success if we can proactively prepare them for situations like this?

If you are changing professions into teaching, welcome! You have entered one of the most noble professions. This book can help support you to create a dynamic classroom right from the start to bring the content you know to a classroom of students who are excited to learn. That takes a whole new set of skills. This could range from knowing what students actually want in a lesson (which we cover in Chapter 3) to knowing how to energize a sleepy class or calm down a wound-up class (which we cover in Chapter 1).

"I know the best way to teach" . . . said no teacher ever. But there are aspects of teaching that work over and over again to get that dynamic classroom. That's what is shared with you in this book.

We, along with all great teachers, know that there are five essential things you do need to know about teaching to thrive and create a dynamic classroom. These are things that might be missed in a teacher prep program, or even things we may have overlooked as our workload piled up after year three or so and now we need a gentle reminder, or just things we gloss over that are ever so important to our effectiveness, well-being, and overall happiness as teachers.

HOW DO I BUILD AN AFFIRMING CLASSROOM COMMUNITY?

Imagine This

When your class walks into your room, you greet each student with a smile. They enter your classroom that has a sign that reads *Welcome to Room 32*, with your name in cursive on the door. There is a buzz of excitement in the air as your students eagerly ask what they will be learning that day, because you know how to make your lessons fun, dynamic, collaborative, relevant, and rigorous all at the same time.

As your students glance around your classroom, they notice that the desks are neatly set in groups of four to five students, which shows they'll have ample opportunities to collaborate with their classmates. You have worked diligently to create a seating chart based on the academic needs of students, along with a few other factors. In your class, all students have an opportunity to succeed because they are seated near somebody who can provide support where needed. As your students start to trust one another, your class of students starts to become a community of learners that begins to form from day one of the school year.

You have a classroom that is not only visually appealing but is somewhere all students are seen, valued, and heard. The books and visuals in your room represent different cultures of the students not only in your classroom but around the world. This includes representation of different races, genders, physicalities, and cultures.

Your students know that if they are struggling with a concept, it means they just don't know it yet. You have taught them this approach, and because of this, engagement stays high through your lessons. They see that you are a role model for this growth mindset as you attend educational conferences with colleagues to improve your own practice and bring the concepts back to your classroom to strengthen your own teaching. You know that teachers are lifelong learners. In addition, you learn teaching strategies from your colleagues and they learn from you. You trust one another.

Yes, some days your class comes to you either wound up or too sleepy to learn optimally, but when this happens you are ready to get the students back on track because you have a toolbox of strategies you can use to quickly get your students ready to learn. And the same goes for those times when students may be off task. You have that toolbox, too. At the heart of the work, deep down, you know all students want to learn.

Believe it or not, you can have this classroom and learning community, but it does take some work. This chapter will support you through creating an affirming classroom community. Creating a supportive and encouraging classroom is the foundation for building a dynamic and thriving classroom.

In this chapter about building an affirmative classroom community, the following questions about building your foundation will be answered:

☐ **How do I create and keep positive vibes in my classroom?**
☐ **How do I make my classroom visually appealing as well as functional?**
☐ **How do I make an effective seating chart?**
☐ **How do I build routines in my classroom?**
☐ **How do I keep and reflect a growth mindset?**
☐ **How do I energize a sleepy class or calm down a wound-up class?**
☐ **How can I ensure engagement and get ahead of off-task behaviors?**
☐ **When and how do I use a behavior contract?**

A classroom is somewhere growth happens. Students grow not only academically in our classrooms but also socially and emotionally. A dynamic classroom is a place where students excel and also feel safe to mess up because mistakes are part of growth. It's a laboratory and a practice field. For learning to happen—real learning, not just task completion—students have to feel emotionally safe, connected with one another as well as with you, like they're in a learning community, and supported in accessing the curriculum and knowing how the classroom runs as a whole. This takes some work from the teacher and behind the scenes. In the majority of classrooms, this all needs to be taught and practiced.

This chapter focuses on how to build an affirming classroom community where students come to our classrooms not only ready to learn but excited and knowing they are valued and supported members. Once we build an affirming classroom community, the magic of teaching content can flourish.

We're confident in saying that most teachers want an affirming classroom community: a classroom where students feel emotionally, socially, and academically supported and encouraged. It starts with us to set this as the tone and still manage to keep clear and consistent behavioral expectations, build routines and norms, and maintain a healthy pace of learning. Creating an affirming classroom community sets students up to help one another create and maintain this type of healthy classroom environment from day one.

How Do I Create and Keep Positive Vibes in My Classroom?

> I think one of the most powerful behavior management techniques is for the students to like you and want to be in your class. I always work on that first, making the class a fun and loving place to be. If students like you and respect you, then they care what you think and want to please you. If you teach through intimidation and fear, you may get temporary results, but at what price?
>
> —MS. PEREZ, CLASSROOM TEACHER

Take a long hard look at what your classroom looks like, what your message is. Ask yourself some reflective questions. Does your classroom represent you and all your students? Did you create an atmosphere that encourages collaboration, makes everyone feel welcome, seen, and heard? Is it a safe space for students to make mistakes? Is it easy for your students to move around and complete projects? These are the questions you can ask yourself when you decide to reimagine your classroom. A home you love most likely has small personal details, and so should a classroom both you and the class can love. We sometimes do not realize how perceptive students are. It's the small things that students notice and that can even describe teachers, like this: "Oh, Ms. Stanley? She was awesome. She used to have cool sticky notes."

When students are in a better mood, they actually access information at a deeper level. It's true! The lower the filter, the more input is allowed to pass through (Gonzalez, 2020). Students who are happy and calm have a lower affective filter, meaning they can learn information faster and more accurately. It's how our brains are wired. This concept is also true for us, but we often don't take the time to think about it. As teachers, it's our responsibility to create this calm and happy environment for our students.

While we wrote this chapter, a friend shared that her son in middle school complained that one of his teachers was always yelling. Her son felt stressed by this teacher's classroom and felt he could not perform at his optimal academic level. After asking a few more questions of her son, she realized that the teacher wasn't yelling out of anger, but it was merely the tone she had in the classroom. It's important that we keep in mind that how we interpret our tone in the classroom may be different from how our students interpret it. Believe it or not, using a sharp and cutting tone to try to engage the students may actually have the opposite effect.

Be mindful of your tone when you speak to the class. Mimic the volume and tone you desire from them. Energy is contagious, so a negative or annoyed teacher usually leads to a negative class. A positive teacher usually can maintain a positive

Agency and Identity

A positive classroom will lend itself to all students wanting to participate, take ownership, and collaborate during the learning process.

Answers to Your Biggest Questions About Creating a Dynamic Classroom

classroom vibe. It's really that simple. Positive energy in the classroom will be crucial, both for you and your students, when there are difficult tasks to get through.

Here are some of our favorite strategies to infuse positive vibes in a classroom to help create an environment conducive to learning:

- Use music to set the mood. Play soft music as students are independently working or even as they are walking into your classroom.
- Start Mondays with five minutes of asking students to share good news with the class. Ask them to share something great that happened over the weekend or the previous week, or something they are looking forward to. If you want to take it a step further, you can have students clap for one another as they share. This helps create a community.
- On Fridays, in addition to your standard homework, consider adding an assignment that can be as simple as "Do something kind for somebody without having them ask you." Then, on Monday, ask kids to write down what happened on a sticky note, perhaps let them share with a neighbor so they can feel good talking about it, and hang the notes on chart paper in your room for a few days. This will create positive vibes in your classroom because students will feel good about themselves. This takes only a few minutes and shows students you genuinely care about them as human beings as well as learners. Doing this every once in a while can have very powerful results.
- Model a positive and calm tone of voice for students.
- Praise positive behaviors when students enter instead of pointing out what students aren't doing. The rest will start to follow suit.
- Make sure class materials are prepared and class is organized before students arrive. This sends a message to students that you care enough about their learning to be prepared and ready to go. An unprepared teacher (and it happens sometimes) often leads to a frustrated teacher, which in turn leads to off-task behaviors and a negative vibe in the classroom.
- When you make your seating chart, seat students who often show negative behavior or attitudes on the sides of the classroom but toward the front so they can stay engaged in the learning. Seat a student who generally exudes positivity in the center and another in the center back. This helps positive energy to be spotlighted and spread. You'd be surprised how a negative student front and center can really spread negative energy to you and also diffuse this energy into the classroom.
- Start off class with a joke. This will get the students engaged, get them laughing, and create positive vibes to start off your lessons, with little effort. Consider keeping a list of jokes ready to go at your desk to use when needed.

✳ Tip #1

Take your class outside if your lesson allows; change the scenery. It's amazing how a little sunshine can lift the mood while keeping the same level of learning.

✳ Tip #2

Find an exercise buddy (or a group) at school or in your personal life to keep yourself at your best. Forming healthy exercise habits will show in your teaching, increase your endorphins, and give you more energy. You and your students will appreciate it. Exercise will increase your positivity.

Keep in Mind
You are the energetic leader of your classroom.

Equity and Access
It's important that we start building a positive classroom for all students from day one. With such academic, cultural, and language-level diversity, students deserve a learning environment where everybody feels emotionally safe and valued.

Tip #3

Record your voice one day while you are doing instruction, and as you listen to it, ask yourself: *Is the tone of my voice sending positivity through the classroom?*

Tip #4

Remember that a class that can laugh together can learn together. Laughter bonds people. A teacher who can get students to laugh can get students to open up and learn.

You may feel the impulse to . . .	Take a deep breath, and try this instead.
Not incorporate team-building activities.	Start slow; team-building activities do not have to take a lot of time, yet help create a sense of community in your classroom. Try integrating a two-minute brain break to begin the idea of movement in the classroom. It's much easier to do these in the beginning of the year than to try to bring back a divided or negative class toward the middle of the year.
Focus on the negative behaviors of a student.	If you've had a tough day with a student, consider making a list of positive aspects about that student. As difficult as that may seem, this will reframe how you approach the student the next day and give you a fresh perspective. If you focus on what the class is doing well, those behaviors will thrive and positivity will spread.
Let a class or student know that you are disappointed when they've had an off day but never let the class or student know when they did well that day.	Make it a point (perhaps put a reminder on your desk that says, "Praise when they do well") to let classes or individuals know when they had a wonderful day. This lets students know you genuinely want them to do well and aren't just waiting to point out their faults. Remember, your classroom is their practice field for life, and everybody makes mistakes sometimes.
Feel uncomfortable if your class is laughing and quickly try to silence it.	If the laughter isn't directed at a student or isn't hurting anybody's feelings, know that laughter can bring a class together and also lowers the affective filter in the students' brains.

Ask Yourself:

- Is my classroom somewhere I'd want to be every day as a student? What can I do to make it more comfortable for all of us?
- Do I feel good when I'm teaching and energized after a class is over? If not, what can I do to change this?
- Do my students know what my laugh sounds like?

Notes

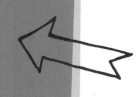

How Do I Make My Classroom Visually Appealing as Well as Functional?

> Trivial details can overwhelm you when organizing your classroom at the beginning of the school year. Make it your own! Do what works for you. For example, if having space on the floor for students to work on their bellies using clipboards is important to you, then be sure to have an area for floor work.

—MS. VAITES, ELEMENTARY SCHOOL TEACHER

Creating a safe, inclusive culture begins with the structure and function of the classroom. What are the messages students, administrators, guests, colleagues, and parents receive as they enter your classroom? Keep things simple. Locations for handing in homework, storing projects, and completing assignments are critical to an efficiently run classroom. Check for areas that may tend to be messy with paper or materials. Ask yourself, is this necessary? Even if it may not bother you so much to have clutter, students simply function at a higher level in a visually organized classroom. Ask yourself, is this something you could store in a file on the computer? In a drawer out of sight? If you cannot find a solution, ask the students for their input; this is their classroom, and they often have the best ideas!

Think of your classroom as a second home. For teachers who live with families or even roommates, a classroom is like a second studio apartment that is all yours. Set it up so it is functional for the students and feels really good to you. View your classroom from the eye level of your students, too, so you can see things from their perspective. What stands out as most important from students' eye level?

Arrange student desks (we recommend groups of four to five) so all students can see the board and the teacher during whole-group instruction and still have room to move around if needed. Some elementary teachers spend a lot of time squatting down or walking on their knees so they can meet every student at eye level, so maintaining lots of space between the groups would be crucial in this case.

Also, remember to check to make sure your projector and all technology around your instructional area works before the school year begins.

Be mindful to create space so students with disabilities can move around the entire room. Try not to have a dedicated space that separates students with mobility considerations. Design your room so all your students can move and join collaborative work groups without barriers. Check for blocked pathways—book bags, materials, or desk configurations that may hinder mobility.

Ask yourself: Can all your students see themselves represented in the classroom? Representation can come in many forms, such as a poster with images of cultural figures who impacted your area of content. Consider playing music that represents multicultural groups throughout the world. Celebrate with food that represents diverse cultures. Invite parents and community members to talk about their experiences and their paths to success. Be wary, however, of cultural appropriation; avoid dressing in costumes, for instance, or working from stereotypes.

Here are some additional ideas to consider as you design your classroom:

- **Bring your personality.** Have fun with this! Students love to know about their teachers. Reserve an area to display pictures or stories representing you, and continue to update it throughout the year. Sprinkle your pets into your curriculum. Share stories about your hobbies. Create a theme around your interests—Harry Potter, sports, superheroes. Bring in a life-size cutout poster of your favorite athlete, actor, or movie. If you enjoy baking, bring in some baked goods. If you are an artist, draw pictures of your students. Bring pictures of you doing your favorite activity and pictures of your family and pets. Think beyond the four walls of the classroom and bring your authentic self to your students! They want to see you as a human being.

- **It doesn't have to break the bank.** Go to garage sales and thrift stores for decorations, books, pictures, furniture, lamps, and shelves. Have students create or bring in items that would help build an inclusive classroom culture. You and your students can have some fun!

- **Incorporate all five senses.** Accent your color schemes with your furniture, wall hangings, rugs, shelves, chairs, couches, and beanbags. Play music that represents cultures around the globe. Play nature sounds that can calm students. You do have to consider allergies, but you can open a window to create airflow. Provide healthy snacks for students to rejuvenate their energy levels. Allow students to use manipulatives. Also, consider providing academic puzzles and games to engage students who finish assignments early. Consider offering items for students who may need to occupy their energy; fidget toys, squeeze balls, pencils and paper for doodling, bungee cords tied on the bottoms of a few chairs, bouncy balls, and swivel chairs are just a few items to consider. It's up to you if this works for you as a teacher.

Tip #1

Create clear, easy-to-follow procedures for handing in materials, assignments, and projects. Make materials accessible for all students.

Tip #2

Empower students to maintain (clean and organize) work areas, shelves, cabinets, games, and so forth.

Tip #3

Provide tissues, hand sanitizer, and unscented lotion.

Tip #4

Keep your classroom clean and organized.

Tip #5

Use air freshener or an essential oil diffuser to keep the room smelling good.

You may feel the impulse to . . .	Take a deep breath, and try this instead.
Not update or even create a wall space that is reserved to reveal your personality or areas of interest. This can be a small space around your desk.	Allow students to get to know you outside of the classroom, building trust, and students will relate to you. Also, you can connect with students by offering stories of how you accomplished goals and your innovative thinking getting around obstacles.
Ignore incorporating one of the five senses into your classroom structure.	Try incorporating one new item a week. You do not have to have your entire design completed before the beginning of the year. It is a work in progress.
Work on aesthetics of your classroom before setting up the learning area and desks.	It's recommended to set up the learning area/s of your classroom and the desk arrangement first, then work your way out to other areas of the room. The rest can wait a bit. The instruction area should be ready to go before day one.

Ask Yourself:

Is my classroom a place where students want to be, and organized so students can learn?

Notes

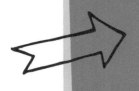

How Do I Make an Effective Seating Chart?

The goal of an effective seating chart is for every group or table to have access to academic success. For small-group instruction or differentiated instruction (both covered in later chapters), groups of students with similar ability levels can be pulled together for periods of time, but this won't be the case for the everyday seating chart.

A seating chart helps your class become a community of learners. This means that students are learning with one another and given the best chance to succeed academically. Learning is, in fact, a social activity, so creating an effective seating chart is a key factor in having a dynamic classroom. A lot of work and consideration go into making an effective seating chart.

A seating chart should ideally be created by day three of the first week of school because students will form bonds with other students seated around them. This is the natural process of a classroom, and of human beings in general. If a seating chart isn't made early in a school year or semester, students will start to bond with those around them, and when you present your seating chart you might come across as the villain when they have to change seats.

Another main purpose of a seating chart is to ensure all students can access the content. For example, a student who is supposed to sit in the front of the class, according to their IEP, may have naturally chosen a seat in the back of the room because they feel more comfortable out of view of other children. But this may not be the most ideal spot for this student. Or two best friends have chosen seats on the side of the classroom so they can whisper to each other while the lesson is taking place. Or a student identified as an English learner may have chosen a seat with all their English learner friends in the back of the room, because that is who they are comfortable with. Or perhaps a student who loves to answer every single question has seated themselves right in the front center so all your attention is on them. It's our job, as teachers and professionals, to look at the data to make a seating chart so every student has the best chance of success in our classroom and a community of learners can start to form.

Instead of leaving student seating to chance, which risks energy spent breaking up groupings and rearranging students, making a purposeful seating chart means you look at students' academic skills, learning disabilities, language barriers, and personality traits and then make a chart from there.

What follows are a few best practices to create a seating chart where all students have the best chance of success in your classroom.

Steps for Creating an Effective Seating Chart:

1 Acquire a list of students with IEPs and 504 plans in your class. This information can often be found on your attendance roster. Remember: students classified as gifted and talented also are classified as having a form

Keep in Mind

A seating chart sketch is best done in pencil so you can change, erase, fix a misspelled name, or swap two seats easily without having to redo the whole thing or ending up with a paper full of correction fluid.

of specialized education and should be spread out as well to balance the academic abilities of your classroom.

2 Find the list of your students classified as English learners (ELs). This information can also often be found on your attendance roster. If this is not the case, try to find the person at your school who can help you obtain this list.

3 Sketch out how you want to arrange your desks. We recommend seating students in groups of four to five. Research suggests this is best for large projects, and "groups of four to five tend to balance the needs for diversity, productivity, active participation, and cohesion" (Centre for Teaching Excellence, n.d.). It will also leave space in your classroom for movement. The most ideal arrangement is one where you and students can move freely around the classroom and get to each group of students and area of the room easily.

4 Place your students with IEPs first on your seating chart sketch, then your students with 504 plans. Spread these students out. Some students may have preferential seating listed in their IEPs, meaning they must sit in the front, in the back, or on the side, depending on their individual needs. This is where they learn best.

5 Spread out your students who are identified as ELs. It's a strategic move to put these students next to very kind, helpful students and, even better, next to another multilingual student who may speak their native language. These students will usually be eager to help a struggling EL student when needed, and the EL student will feel comfortable with them. It's a win-win. This makes a difference in how many directions you are pulled during a lesson. It can be helpful to have a brief and private conversation with the helpful student at some point in the beginning of the year, too.

6 Spread out your students who may have AVID designations.

7 Spread out your students identified as GATE (Gifted and Talented Education).

8 Spread out your general education students. This information can also be found on your attendance roster.

It's important that you don't mark up the seating chart with IEP and other ability-descriptive labels, but you do want to be able to identify these students when you are teaching so you can support them as needed throughout a lesson. In other words, Johnny does not need to know which students at his table have an IEP or are classified as ELs, but as a teacher, you do. Consider using different-color highlighters on student names so you know what those colors mean but a student who happens to glance at the chart will not.

If you wait two days or so to make a seating chart and do some sort of icebreaker activity, you'll be able to see the personalities of the students. When you identify high-energy students who are eager to raise their hands in the first two days, you'll want to seat one of them in the front center group of the class and one in the back center. Their energy and enthusiasm will most often radiate out into the classroom.

This goes for students who seem less enthusiastic, too. You usually want to try to seat them on the side so their energy doesn't radiate out. Place at least one vocal student at each table group or area of the room. These students will reveal themselves in the first few days if you do student-centered activities (e.g., group work, icebreakers, activities on their feet). Do at least one of these the first few days, and make notes (in code) on a student roster of the vocal, happy, and negative students. This will help you make a seating chart.

Keep in Mind

Think of a seating chart as another limb on your body until you know all the students' names confidently. Consider having it on a clipboard and holding it whenever you circulate around the classroom so you can always refer to students by name. (However, plan to know your students' names as soon as possible!)

In middle and high school, you may change the desks one day to have a dynamic lesson, such as a Socratic seminar, a debate, a circle meeting, or a horseshoe for presentations. This is great, but the students know they will always come back to their home base seating when that lesson or activity is over. Changing up the seating for a portion of a classroom or for a day or two can create new excitement in a lesson. If you need to do a few (just a few) swaps later, you can, and the sooner the better. Just make sure you still have students classified as IEP, EL, and GATE evenly spread out in your class.

Figure 1.1 This image shows an example of a seating chart that keeps students' academic levels, languages, and personalities in mind to give them the best chance at success.

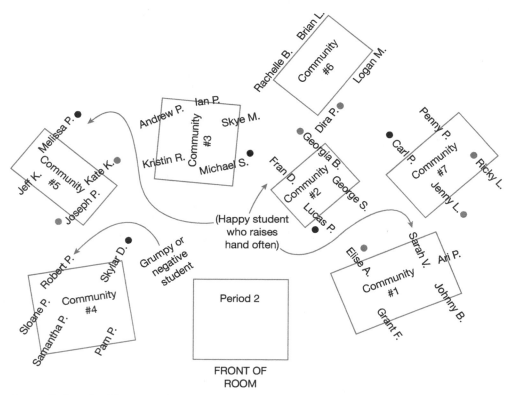

Source: Pariser, *Real Talk About Classroom Management* (2018).

You may feel the impulse to . . .	Take a deep breath, and try this instead.
Make a seating chart purely based on behavior without looking at academic and language levels of the students, and then hope for the best.	Use the steps above to make an effective and proactive seating chart that gives each student a chance to succeed academically.
Consult with the teacher from the year before so they can give you a heads-up on the students who may exhibit challenging behaviors.	Give students the benefit of the doubt and know students change dramatically from year to year. Every student deserves a fresh start. Think of it like this: If you had an "off" year teaching and happened to change schools the next year, would you want your old principal calling your new principal to let them know how much you messed up? Wouldn't you want the chance at a fresh start?

You may feel the impulse to . . .	Take a deep breath, and try this instead.
Move the students who exhibit challenging behavior to the front center of the room.	Try to refrain from moving the student who exhibits challenging behavior to the front of the room. This can sometimes increase their anxiety. The goal is to eventually help their strengths shine in the classroom. Try seating them with a peer who is patient and willing to mentor them.

Keep in Mind

Students who feel comfortable helping one another and working together with one another's strengths build a community of learners in a classroom of students who are not entirely dependent on you.

Great Resources

- Opinion article: Behan, K. (2019, August 17). Create a culture, not a classroom: Why seating charts matter for student success. *EdSurge.* https://bit.ly/3pRn1XY

- Website: *Classroom seating arrangements.* (2017). Yale Poorvu Center for Teaching and Learning. https://poorvucenter.yale.edu/ClassroomSeating Arrangements

- Book: Pariser, S. (2018). *Real Talk About Classroom Management* (pp. 22–30). Corwin.

Ask Yourself:

Have I spread out all the students so every pair/group/table has equal opportunity to succeed with the learning and have somebody at their table who can help them if needed?

Notes

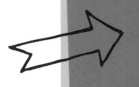

How Do I Build Routines in My Classroom?

If you've ever covered a colleague's classroom, you know that you can tell if that teacher has established routines for the students. Even when the teacher isn't there, the students know what to do. They enter the classroom a particular way; they go to their seats and start their beginning-of-class routine without much prompting. There's a sense of calmness, and students are comfortable with how the class runs. This type of classroom, one that runs like a well-oiled machine, shows that the teacher set structures early and was consistent in implementation. Yes, it takes work and, more important, practice behind the scenes to get here, but it's so worth it. Setting routines and structures early almost guarantees a successful year.

> Therefore, the most important thing a teacher can provide in the classroom during the first week of school is CONSISTENCY. Classroom practices and procedures must be predictable and consistent.
>
> —HARRY WONG AND ROSEMARY T. WONG, *THE FIRST DAYS OF SCHOOL* (2009)

A dynamic classroom that runs smoothly has established routines and procedures early in the school year. Routines should be taught as early as possible in the school year, usually in the first few days of school. The beginning of the school year is when both good and bad habits are formed. This is true for both students and teachers.

A routine is something that happens every day with a purpose. Having routines creates a sense of calmness and comfort for both you and your students. Having established routines also allows you to focus on the content during the day rather than repeating yourself over and over again for low-level instructions.

Make your routines simple, and try your best not to change or skip them for lack of time. This will prevent student confusion. For example, if the first 10 minutes of class are always structured where students take out their notebooks, answer a question, then take out their reading logs and place their homework on their desks as they begin reading, it is extremely important that you do this daily. Yes, it's tempting to skip a part of this established routine for the sake of time some days, but once you or the students start cutting corners with routines, it's a slippery slope and the students will forget the routines quickly.

In the beginning of the school year, practice routines in class daily. Movement creates muscle memory so students will be more likely to remember how to do it. The approach to practicing routines should include something like charades or a competition or some element of fun. Consistency is key. We can't expect students to know how to do it if we don't teach it. The more consistently you do the routine, the faster the students will learn it.

Remember to praise students when they follow the routine, instead of focusing only on criticizing when they mess it up. This is a more powerful way to make a routine stick. Consider having the important routines posted around the room, too, as students are learning them, for your visual learners. Pictures of students doing the routine can be powerful.

> Hey, it's not too late! If you are coming into a classroom as a long-term substitute or a teacher midyear, adjust the routines or even make new ones as they work for you. Students can learn routines quickly.

Structure the first 10 minutes of class with the same routine so students will be in control of their responsibilities when they first come into the room. Have that routine posted somewhere or placed on your document camera as they enter each day so you can just point to it if a student needs a reminder. You'll need a few minutes to take attendance and address daily "housekeeping" items, so if a student comes into the room and claims they don't know what to do, you can simply point to where the routine is displayed instead of repeating yourself.

It is crucial that we remember that different families have different norms of behavior at home. We have to teach the behaviors that are optimal for creating a community of learners instead of expecting students to come to us with these behaviors already. When we meet each student where they are and give them support to access each routine, we're creating an equitable classroom environment. It is important to avoid judging what students learn or do not learn at home. This could look like having a private conversation with a student about a particular routine or providing a tool or pathway to help them be successful. If, for example, Evon has trouble remembering what to do in the first 10 minutes of class, you can provide a reminder checklist that she tapes to the front of her notebook. Or if Eduardo constantly forgets his notebook at home, you can provide a space in your room where he can store it. The belief that every student can learn routines that make your class run smoothly is one that the greatest teachers hold.

Keep in Mind

Think of fire drills: They're physically practiced with students consistently so they are routine for them. The same should be done with our classroom routines.

Some beginning-of-class routines could look like this:

Routines and Procedure	Grade Level
Entering and leaving the classroom	K–8
Getting a drink, going to the restroom, sharpening a pencil, how to line up	K–6
When and how to hand in work	K–12
Technology—how to check out, plug in/charge, acceptable websites	K–12
Where homework is indicated on board	1–12
Signing books out of the classroom library	K–12
Structure and what to expect of first and last 5 to 10 minutes of class	K–12

Agency and Identity

Students can take initiative in creating the posters for the routine. Ask them to suggest adjustments that meet their personal learning needs, too.

You may feel the impulse to . . .	Take a deep breath, and try this instead.
Not have students practice the routine.	Two weeks into the semester, begin the class by having the students write the criteria and rationale for the routine. Consider having the students role-play an example and a non-example of the routine or even take pictures of examples and non-examples of the routine. Make it fun!
Practice only once, even if they just "sort of" got it.	Make a game or a contest out of it. Have a student show how *not* to follow the routine. Charades work well, too. Have fun with it!
Discipline or scold the students when they mess up the taught routine.	Consider offering small rewards when students get the routines correct as they are learning them.
Skip a routine some days due to lack of time (e.g., skipping the routine for the first 10 minutes of class to do something else).	Consistency is key to learning a routine, and daily practice is a must. Students will unlearn a routine just as fast as they learn it.

Ask Yourself:

How can I structure the routine for the first 10 minutes of class, and how can it be posted visually so students can see it front and center when they enter my classroom?

Notes

How Do I Keep and Reflect a Growth Mindset?

> The secret of change is to focus all of your energy not on struggling with the old but on building the new.
>
> —DAN MILLMAN, *WAY OF THE PEACEFUL WARRIOR* (2006, P. 105)

Growth mindset is a term you will hear often in the teaching profession. According to Stanford professor Carol Dweck (2016), a growth mindset **describes people who believe that their success depends on time and effort**.

Simply put, people with a growth mindset feel their skills and intelligence can be improved with effort and persistence. People who embrace a growth mindset see effort as the path to mastery. The opposite of a growth mindset is a fixed mindset. A fixed mindset can be detrimental to your success as a teacher. For example, thinking you are not good at facilitating group work is a fixed mindset. Thinking you are not good at facilitating group work *just yet* is a growth mindset.

A growth mindset can be beneficial to both educators and students. Keeping a growth mindset is crucial in developing as an educator because the profession, the world, and our students are constantly growing and changing, and keeping a growth mindset helps us stay motivated and resilient.

Teachers are often known to "teach in silos," which means we stay isolated from one another and mostly confined to our classrooms. This may naturally happen with so many tasks to complete in our classrooms and the fact that we keep to our classrooms when we are teaching. However, breaking out of your silo and learning from a colleague can be a powerful way to keep a growth mindset. Consider asking a teacher whom you and the students admire if you can observe a lesson or even a portion of a lesson during your prep period. You'd be surprised what you can learn by watching a colleague for just a portion of a class.

Keep in Mind

The key is to keep the word *yet* in mind: "I don't know how to do that . . . yet . . . but I will keep trying."

As educators, when we take on a growth mindset, we can also reflect that mindset to our students. Our students will see that we are constantly growing as educators, are not afraid to try new activities and types of lessons in the classroom, and understand that teaching is a lifelong journey of constant self-improvement.

Phrases that reflect a growth mindset to our students:

- We don't know how to do this yet, but we will!

- Great effort!

- I see you are working diligently on that!

- I just don't know how to do it yet.

- Mistakes are all part of the growth.

The phrases we communicate to students in our words and written feedback can instill a culture of growth mindset in our classrooms.

Here are some ideas to think about as you consider how to keep a growth mindset:

Equity and Access

If there is a population of students you'd like to know more about how to serve as a teacher, scope out those webinars, books, and speakers that specialize in that topic. Knowledge is power, and it will make you a stronger teacher to serve all students.

Keep in Mind

Twitter is especially helpful for teachers. Many of the best teachers out there use this forum to share tips, ask questions, or learn new best practices from one another.

- **Professional development:** When you learn a new strategy, offer to present your ideas to your team, school, or district-level staff. Teachers and administrators are always looking for new methods of teaching. Online professional development is easy to view live or on demand. Ask colleagues or your administrator for any local opportunities, and take advantage of opportunities provided by your district or school.
- **Education conferences and organizations:** Attending education conferences provides opportunities to network, attain new ideas and strategies, and gain fresh perspectives. Also, you can bring back new ideas to your school and present what you learned to your team. Consider presenting at a conference, too, to share your own knowledge and great ideas. Often, large districts have grants for travel costs, and perhaps you'll get to see a new city, too. Subscribing to newsletters and blogs of education organizations is an efficient way to stay in the know about upcoming conferences in your area, as well as best practices.
- **Book clubs:** Forming a book club with colleagues not only pushes your learning but is a great way to connect with your colleagues. You can choose from some of the "Great Resources" in this book to get started!
- **Education webinars:** Thanks to the COVID-19 pandemic, we are now more at ease with webinar platforms, which are a great way to connect with educational experts worldwide. And more organizations, publishers, and educators are presenting webinars all the time. Social media is a good way to keep up with what's available.
- **Graduate school:** Higher education exposes you to working with current research, you can network with colleagues from different districts and potentially other states, and it positions you for promotions.
- **Community engagement:** Working with community programs will connect you with your neighborhood school or local community, and it builds a sense of community among you, your students, and their families.
- **Education podcasts:** Podcasts are perfect for busy teachers. They are a great way to improve your practice and hear from other teachers who are exploring topics in education or perhaps even talking about the same issues you may be having in the classroom. It's often refreshing to hear from teachers who are not at your school to gain a wider perspective of education. You can listen while at the gym, while washing dishes, or whenever else you have a moment.
- **Facing fears:** When you feel yourself wanting to participate in something that may be outside your comfort zone, this is an indicator you should go for it! Think about the thrill of accomplishing something you didn't think you could do but had a burning desire to try—it's a great feeling!
- **Asking for help:** Growth mindset is admitting when you need some guidance. Remember that it is not a sign of stupidity or ignorance to ask questions. This is what we teach our students, and this is how we grow. There is not one teacher who has the answer to every question.

Tip #1

Designate a time during every week to read an article or blog post. Subscribe to education blogs written by educators you admire.

Tip #2

Listen to an education podcast, read an article, or watch a video as you exercise or commute to work.

Tip #3

Be in the know about which professional development opportunities count toward gaining credits for a possible pay-scale increase (some schools do this). Check with your human resources department.

You may feel the impulse to . . .	Take a deep breath, and try this instead.
Tell yourself you do not have time to read articles or a book on teacher development.	Consider reading a blog or a shorter article. You can even listen to a podcast as you are exercising.
Refrain from having a growth mindset your first few years of teaching because you have too much to do.	Know that your first few years teaching are when you can form bad habits that become hard to break. So this is exactly when keeping a growth mindset should be one of your priorities.
Wait for somebody to tell you about a conference.	Take initiative! Stay subscribed to education organizations that interest you, and let administration know when larger conferences come up that you'd like to attend. Often, administration will be open to sending a group of teachers to a conference together to strengthen a department or grade level.

Recommended Professional Organizations

- AMLE (Association for Middle Level Education)
- ISTE (International Society for Technology in Education)
- ASCD (Association of Supervision and Curriculum Development)
- NEA (National Education Association)
- NCTE (National Council for Teachers of English)
- ILA (International Literacy Association)
- NCTM (National Council for Teachers of Math)
- NCSS (National Council for the Social Studies)
- NSTA (National Science Teachers Association)

Many of these organizations offer state and/or local chapters, too.

Great Resources

- Book: Dweck, C. S. (2016). *Mindset*. Ballantine Books.
- Video: Carol Dweck TED Talks, available on YouTube.

Educational podcasts to try:

- *The Staff Room Podcast*
- *The Shake Up Learning Show*
- *Teachers on Fire*
- *The Cult of Pedagogy Podcast*
- *Teacher Saves World!*

Ask Yourself:

Are there areas of growth I avoid? Make a list of items you would like to try, and set a goal to try one each month.

Notes

_____
_____
_____
_____
_____
_____
_____
_____
_____
_____
_____
_____
_____
_____
_____
_____

How Do I Energize a Sleepy Class or Calm Down a Wound-Up Class?

Students of any age are unpredictable balls of energy. Their minds and bodies are going through intense changes, they may have consumed a handful of sugar for breakfast, or perhaps they had trouble sleeping the night before because their younger sibling kept them awake. As strange as it seems, one day they can be bouncing off the walls as they walk into your classroom, and the next day they can be asleep on their desk before class starts. However, the learning must go on!

Use your discretion to determine which of the activities can be tweaked for your grade level and for the learners in your class. Have fun with it!

If your students are too wound up to start the class (after PE, lunch, etc.), you can try the following:

1   Play relaxing music and start the class with a few minutes of independent reading.
2   Start class with a 4-7-8 breathing exercise. This breathing exercise has been proven to calm and clear the mind. Close your mouth and inhale for four seconds. Hold your breath for seven seconds, then exhale out of your mouth for eight seconds. Repeat a few times.
3   A simple game of Simon Says can redirect a bit of the energy so they become focused on you and burn off some steam.
4   Place a visually appealing treat (cookie, candy, etc.) on the document camera, and zoom in really close. Take the treat off of the camera and hide it in your desk. Calmly give the class directions on how they can "win" the treat if they follow all the beginning-of-class procedures. Perhaps they get a ticket of some sort when you see they are ready to learn, meaning they've written down their homework, they are quiet and focused, and they have their notebooks out, ready to go, and are waiting patiently. Students can write their names on the tickets and give them back to you. Then draw a name from your pile of tickets, and that student can have a treat. This will focus them quickly, as they will want to earn that ticket!
5   Make sure your voice is calm, and speak a little slower than usual. If you have a microphone, try using that instead of raising your voice. A screaming teacher creates an anxious class.
6   Instead of starting class by raising your voice, simply have the start-of-class directions written large enough for the class to see, or have it projected, and point to it. Be one step ahead of your class when they arrive.
7   Read a picture book or, even better, play an audio chapter of a book (almost any chapter of a book being read aloud can be found on YouTube). There is something really soothing about listening to a book being read by somebody other than their teacher. This also gives you a bit of a vocal break so you can put your full self into the lesson.

Keep in Mind

It's helpful to keep this list of strategies (and your own strategies you'll discover and add to it) taped somewhere near your desk so you can pull an idea quickly on the fly. If you keep it at eye level or higher, it can't get covered by papers on your desk.

If your students are dragging their feet or half asleep as you are starting class, you can try the following:

1. Play upbeat music softly as the students are entering class or as they are working independently. You may see students start to bob their heads a bit and perk up.

2. Depending on the grade level, a simple game of Simon Says can get students up and moving (yes, it can work both ways).

3. Try a game called Stand if You. It's simple: The teacher makes a statement, and students stand if it applies to them. This will get the blood flowing and also works as a movement activity during a natural transition in a long lesson. Weave in personal and academic material you just taught, if you feel like it. Examples:

   - Stand if you have more than one brother.
   - Stand if you know the difference between a simile and a metaphor.
   - Stand if you have ever fallen off a skateboard.

4. If a class repeatedly comes to you sleepy (e.g., Period 1 at 7:30 a.m.), try starting the class with an on-your-feet engaging activity, like visiting stations all around your room or doing a quick trivia challenge on your content (perhaps for a small treat). It's helpful to have these materials (debate questions, etc.) ready to grab from somewhere in your desk or an area of your room so you can wake the class up with little delay!

5. Try a debate or "would you rather" activity (pop culture or current events make engaging topics) to get students moving and talking to one another. The more students on their feet, the better. Perhaps have a running list of engaging debate or "would you rather" questions ready to go and taped near your desk to use quickly if needed. If you can tie the questions into what you are teaching, even better.

An engagement trick is if students come in wound up, you could say, "Okay, we can either go right into the learning or play a game first." Students will (almost) always choose the game option. Little do they know it's actually an activity to get them ready for learning. Then you can do Simon Says, Stand if You, or the like, and they will think it was their idea. This is also empowering for students and will either wake them up or calm them down, depending on what they need. In elementary and middle, you can call it a game. In high school, you can do a debate (pop culture or current events) or some other engaging activity that gets them moving and talking to one another.

It is helpful to keep a list of both energizing and calming activities hung up (so it doesn't get lost in the shuffle of papers) near your desk to refer to quickly if needed. Our minds become so full of everything we have to remember during the day that the list can remind you of all the tools you have in your teacher toolbox.

Helpful tips for those one to two students who seem to never come into class ready to learn:

Tip #1

If one student in particular is "bouncing off the walls," send them on a five-minute walk around campus or give them an errand, like delivering a note to another teacher or walking something to the office. Set a timer so they are accountable for coming back quickly.

Equity and Access

If you have students who are in a wheelchair in your class, adjust the Stand if You game to Raise Your Hand if You or Clap Twice if You.

Keep in Mind

There may be a deeper issue as to why a student is falling asleep in your Period 1 class every day. Check in with a counselor to see what other supports a student can receive.

Tip #2

If one to two students consistently come into the classroom not ready to learn, consider starting them on a behavior contract.

Tip #3

Schedule a 1:1 with these students individually during a lunch meeting or other set time. If the students do redirect their behavior, praise them for it with private words or a short note. Plan to check in regularly to build a relationship; positive relationships go a long way toward engagement, positive behavior, and learning.

You may feel the impulse to . . .	Take a deep breath, and try this instead.
Raise your voice at the class to startle them or shame them into being quiet.	Start class with a calming voice, and write out directions on the document camera so students can redirect themselves. Have a calm talk with the class a few minutes after they have quieted down about your expectations for how they enter class.
Keep teaching even when students are about to fall asleep at their desks (or perhaps even are sleeping on their desks).	If it is one or two students, gently tap their desks as you walk by them while teaching. If it is most of the class, do an activity that requires them to move (see suggestions above) when there is a natural break in the lesson to get that blood flowing! This also shows you value that they are learning, not just getting through the information.

Ask Yourself:

- (In the beginning of a class) Is my classroom of students ready to learn for the day, or should I do one of the above strategies?
- (In the middle of a class, especially a long block period) Does my class of students need a boost of energy? If so, try one of the strategies above and see the difference it can make!

Notes

How Do I Energize a Sleepy Class or Calm Down a Wound-Up Class?

27

COMMUNITY

How Can I Ensure Engagement and Get Ahead of Off-Task Behaviors?

Off-task behavior can manifest in multiple forms—sleeping student, talkative student, sudden outbursts, or teasing. You get the idea . . . and you've likely seen these behaviors in a classroom. When these types of behaviors arise, there is a good chance students are bored or, on the flip side, intimidated by the material. Or perhaps they know the material, but they do not want to look interested due to negative peer pressure. There are a multitude of reasons for off-task behavior. Ultimately, the student is not engaged and may be disrupting the learning environment.

How do we get ahead of off-task behaviors? Engage the students with simple strategies that can be done with all learners throughout the lesson. The following strategies keep you one or two steps ahead of your class and keep engagement high.

Something as simple as bringing your authentic self to the classroom can get engagement going before, during, or even after a lesson. For example, you could share a story with them about when you lack interest in something; this will build trust, and students will relate with you.

Solutions to build engagement and prevent off-task behaviors:

- **Proximity:** Slowly move away from the front of the room and stand close to the student; this is a nonverbal cue that can prompt the student to resume their task.
- **Asking questions:** Engage your class using open-ended questions as you are teaching. Have students discuss with a partner and then share out.
- **Adjusting pacing:** Make sure to be aware of your students' behavior. If they are sleeping, speed up your instruction. If they have blank stares, this may indicate you are going too fast.
- **Limiting direct instruction time:** Consider chunking your lessons into 10-minute increments—10 minutes for direct instruction, 10 minutes for you and your students to work together, 10 minutes for partner or small-group work, and 10 minutes for independent work.
- **Integrating movement:** Even three minutes of exercise can engage their minds and bodies. Better yet if you can link the movement with curriculum to review material.
- **Student interests:** Incorporate their interests into your lessons.
- **Humor:** Have fun with the students. Relate a personal story that conveys empathy or a story about how you may have had trouble with particular aspects of the content. (Note: Make sure your humor is not sarcastic; this can be detrimental to your students' self-esteem, and some students, especially younger children or those who show neurodiversity, may not understand sarcasm.)

- **Being prepared for early finishers:** Have something ready for students who complete a task ahead of others. For more on early finishers, please see Chapter 3.
- **Peer teaching:** Give your students opportunities to teach one another. They love to talk, and they learn a great deal more hearing it from more than one person, especially when it is from their peers.
- **Call-and-response:** This can help you get students' attention quickly. The teacher says a common phrase and the students finish it. This is most effective when it is taught and practiced in the first few days of school as a routine.
  - Example: Teacher: Macaroni and cheese . . . Students: Everybody freeze!
  - Example: Teacher: And a hush fell across the room . . . Students: Shhh! (For more creative call-and-response ideas, scan the QR code in the margin.
- **Consistent structure:** Structure the first and last 10 minutes of your class so students know exactly how they begin and end class.
- **Aural cues:** Use a chime to get students' attention so you don't have to yell (yelling creates or can set off particularly anxious students).
- **Visual cues:** Post routines around the room so students have visual cues and you don't have to repeat yourself.
- **Being one step ahead:** Pass out papers and materials to groups *before* class if possible. Often, taking too much time to pass out papers during a lesson can disrupt the flow of a lesson, and students can become disengaged.

Creative Call-and-Response Ideas (Watson, 2014)

https://thecornerstoneforteachers.com/50-fun-call-and-response-ideas-to-get-students-attention/

To read a QR code, you must have a smartphone or tablet with a camera. We recommend that you download a QR code reader app that is made specifically for your phone or tablet brand.

Tip #1

When engaging your students with open-ended questioning, use ice-pop sticks with their names on them or draw their names from a container. Or you can use a spinner with class names on it, roll a dice, or pull a card with a number on it that correlates to a student. Make participating fun!

Tip #2

Remember, if a student is showing signs that they are struggling to voice the answer, give them a break and allow someone else to answer your question. A student who struggles academically in class may shut down by putting their head on the desk.

Tip #3

Consider creating with your students hand signals accompanied by voice signals for students to follow. This will limit your talking and hold students accountable to pay close attention. If you want to be courageous, try not talking but relying on signals from the entire class to make it fun when they are learning them. Students love to decipher your improv skills as well!

You may feel the impulse to . . .	Take a deep breath, and try this instead.
Demand that a student refocus.	Give the student choices. These choices could be regarding their behavior. Walk away after the choice is given to them privately. This allows the student to "save face" in front of other students and keeps your relationship with that student.
Use sarcasm for humor.	Ask yourself if this is going to degrade or embarrass a student.
Use self-deprecating humor.	Ask yourself if this paints a positive role model for your students. A little self-deprecating humor is great for students to relate to you, but steer clear of using it all the time.

Ask Yourself:

Which of these strategies work best for the learners in my classroom?

Notes

When and How Do I Use a Behavior Contract?

One of the colloquial definitions of insanity is "doing the same things over and over again and expecting a different result." When we hope a student's consistent off-task behavior will magically change, we are unfortunately in this mindset. Often, it just gets worse if not addressed early on. In this chapter, we have discussed proactive strategies to increase engagement, building routines or providing structure and consistency, and how to address off-task behaviors. However, in your first few weeks of school, you will notice this is not enough for a few students. You will likely have one or two students who are disrupting the flow of the lesson, distracting other students, or perhaps just not being that nice to you. Also, your classroom consequences, such as calling home, simply will not work for these students and the same behaviors will happen again and again. These behaviors need to be eliminated immediately, because they can become contagious.

This is where a behavior contract comes in. A behavior contract is for any student who is disrupting the lesson on a consistent basis. The earlier you start a behavior contract, the better. A behavior contract is a temporary scaffold to help that student reach the same behavior expectations as the other students. Sometimes behavior contracts are viewed as a punishment, when in fact they should be seen as something the student *gets* to do. When the student does well for three to four weeks in a row on a behavior contract, they should be taken off that contract because they are ready to fly, so to speak, on their own. If a behavior contract is pitched right, the student will want to be on the contract because it gives them a reason to follow the behavioral expectations of the classroom, when they might not have had a reason to before.

A good rule of thumb is to have only one to three students from each period maximum on a behavior contract, and only if needed. Behavior contracts take time and a bit of work from the teacher but are well worth the payoffs of not having extreme off-task behaviors from the same student, defiance, and a particular student interrupting the lesson and learning on a daily basis.

Tip #1

Behavior contracts should always be co-created with the student.

Tip #2

Behavior contracts should be pitched as an opportunity for the student to be able to succeed in class.

Tip #3

Students should be able to choose their own "rewards" (perhaps from a list you provide).

Tip #4

Students should hold on to their own behavior contracts.

Tip #5

Urge students not to let other students know they are on a behavior contract (or every student would want to be on one and other students may see it as unfair). It's a scaffold this particular student needs.

Tip #6

In the contract, have only one to three desired behaviors (observable and written in the positive) for the student, and grade the student daily at the end of class. Often students who exhibit challenging behavior also have difficulty multitasking and focusing, so addressing one behavior at a time may be the best strategy. Ask the student what they think they earned for the day. For example, a desired behavior could be "completes all classwork" or "talks at appropriate times," rather than "does not sleep in class" or "does not shout out."

Steps for how to implement a behavior contract:

1. Have a brief talk with the student privately (if you have a co-teacher, be sure to invite them, too) about why they might not be performing so well in class. If you can, pitch it like "Remember when you had a B in the class? Didn't that feel better than the F you have now?" Show you believe that they can make a comeback.

2. Co-create a behavior contract with them and point out the three behaviors that can get them back on track. Let them know this particular contract might be different from other contracts they have been on before (if they are an older student). Let them pick their rewards if they make their goal for the week. Perhaps even let them personalize the contract by choosing an image to put on the front of it, something that interests them, and choosing a font for their name. They should have some choice in personalizing parts of it.

3. Show the student how the points add up each week. Remember, students will not be perfect right away; it's a progression. This means that the first week perhaps they just need to earn 60 percent of the points, the second week 70 percent, the third week 80 percent, and the last week 90 percent. This gives them confidence they can do it. You also want them to earn the contract reward the first week, or they might give up on it and you are back to square one. Remember, if a student does not earn the contract reward the first week, simply lower the percentage and start them on week one again. So instead of trying to earn 60 percent of the points, they try for 50 percent starting the next Monday. If a student earns week one, then earns week two, then happens to mess up and not earn week three, simply start them over again on week three the next Monday.

4. Go over the consequences if they don't earn the percentage of points they need each week. A phone call home is a powerful consequence and saves you time because now you have to do only one phone call a week instead of multiple phone calls. Contrarily, a positive phone call home can also be a favorite reward for students. Who doesn't want a positive phone call home on a Friday?

Agency and Identity

Behavior contracts flip the script on how we support students who often fall through the cracks of our traditional systems. Students are now in charge of what is expected of them and take ownership of it daily.

5 Make sure the student signs the contract, and feel free to even shake on it.

6 Start the contract on Monday. Let the student know that you really hope they do well!

Possible rewards:

- Technology time during lunch
- Technology time during lunch, with a friend
- Microwave popcorn
- *America's Funniest Home Videos* or another favorite show during lunch
- Teacher's assistant for the day
- Field trip
- Greeter privilege for a guest speaker
- Cool pencils/school supplies
- Ice pops (these clean up easier than ice cream)
- Ice-pop party with a friend (the following week they can bring two friends)
- Lunch with the teacher (works well in elementary school)

(Note: Any of these rewards can be celebrated with a friend to make it an even bigger reward the next week. Example: Week one—ice pops and technology, week two—ice pops with a friend and technology, week three—ice pops with two friends and technology, etc.)

Figure 1.2 Behavior contract example 1.

Jamica's ENGLISH CLASS
Contract

Week of _____
(date)

Week 1 GOAL Percent to reach reward: 60% = 9 boxes marked with a 3, 4, or 5

	Monday	Tuesday	Wednesday	Thursday	Friday
Be polite to all adults in room with words and actions	5				
Follow directions the first time asked	4				
Stay focused without sound disruptions during instruction time	5				

*A LOST CONTRACT RESULTS IN A 1 FOR THAT ENTIRE DAY

5 = 80–100%   4 = 60–80%   3 = 40–60%   2 = 20–40%   1 = 0–20%

Source: Behavior contract created by Dr. Orletta Nguyen.

Keep in Mind

It's always best to have the launch meeting about the contract with the student on a Friday and start it on a Monday. That way, the student has a fresh start after the meeting.

Keep in Mind

When a student earns the reward for the week, it's important that this reward is given at the beginning of the next week so students can start to trust you and be motivated to work for the next week. So if a student earns their first week on Friday, technology time during lunch with candy should happen the next Monday or Tuesday.

Figure 1.3 Behavior contract example 2.

I, _____, agree to the following contract. If I am successful I will receive the weekly prize. If I am unsuccessful, I will receive a negative phone call home. I will give this contract to Ms. Pariser at the END of every class to sign.

        PRIZES!!

WEEK 1: Technology time during lunch with candy
WEEK 2: Technology time during lunch with candy AND popcorn
WEEK 3: Technology time during lunch with friend with candy, popcorn, and soda
WEEK 4: Technology time during lunch with two friends with candy and popcorn

Source: Behavior contract created by Dr. Orletta Nguyen.

Notes

Recap: Try This Tomorrow

Each of these strategies takes very little prep and can help you build an affirming classroom community.

- Consider having an area in the room with student pictures (academic as well as nonacademic), and rotate them out every so often.
- Practice class routines with games or charades for student buy-in and to make it fun.
- Have desks in groups of four to five, and make sure all students can see you and the board.
- Subscribe to an education-focused blog, organization, or podcast that can give you ideas as a teacher.
- When students first enter your classroom, praise the positive behaviors you see from them.
- Instead of starting class by raising your voice, simply have the start-of-class directions written large enough for the class to see, or have them projected, and point to them. Be one step ahead of your class when they arrive.
- Pass out papers before a lesson begins.
- Play relaxing music as students are reading or working independently.

Notes

chapter TWO

HOW DO I KEEP STUDENTS AT THE CENTER?

Imagine This

Your students trust you as a content teacher and also with their social and emotional needs. The students in your classes like and respect one another. You have helped create this environment. Students feel safe with you, and because of that, they are eager to learn from you as well as one another. Behind the scenes of the content and classroom environment lies the infrastructure of a classroom that has strong, healthy, and thriving student–teacher and student–student relationships. Yes, some days your students have minor conflicts with one another because they are human. The strength of your classroom lies in the assurance that they always come back together and learning is at the forefront.

Your classroom is built on strong relationships. To build these relationships, you have invested time and also developed ways to do so efficiently. This means that although you may not get to touch base with each student individually daily, all your students feel seen and heard. You have also made sure that your students have had opportunities to build relationships with one another as they work in collaborative groups and even lead and teach one another in group projects. You have a strong belief that every single student wants to and can learn. Not only do your students like and respect you as a teacher and a human being, but you stand out to them from other teachers they have had.

You have systems in place to support students who show signs of academic struggle because you care about your students and don't want anyone to fall behind. The students know and appreciate this, and they value you as their teacher.

Your classroom expectations and management system are designed so they are equitable and just for every learner and set every student up for success, not only in your classroom but in the real world.

When somebody walks into your classroom, they notice that the students are doing a majority of the talking and you are a facilitator guiding them as they collaborate. The students are doing most of the "work," learning the content in a powerful way and showing confidence, content knowledge, enthusiasm, and engagement. Students in your classroom enjoy the process of learning.

Every student in the classroom feels connection and a sense of belonging. Behind the scenes, you've put systems in place to make sure students who are English learners have the tools and strategies they need to succeed and gain a sense of value and belonging. Every student is seen and heard and feels valued in your classroom. You believe they all have something important to say, and they feel this.

Your students understand why you have these expectations, and they have also been given a chance to have fun learning the classroom behavioral expectations with activities such as charades and role-playing. The classroom is not you versus them; it's about "us." Your students value the structure of your learning environment and are on their way to becoming a community of learners.

Imagine this as your reality.

A thriving classroom has strong teacher–student as well as student–student relationships at its core. In fact, it's been found that classrooms where teachers report having strong teacher-to-student relationships have 31 percent fewer behavior disruptions (Marzano et al., 2003). When you have more than 30 students, forming relationships with each one can be challenging. We'll show you efficient ways to do this so you can connect often with each student.

It's important to keep in mind that many of the students who are sitting in your classroom are what we call "connection kids." This means they have to like you to learn from you. You'll also have students who need to overcome learning, language, and social barriers to academically succeed in your classroom. This is when it's time to roll up our teacher sleeves and get to work. We need to keep all students in the center of our thinking and the center of decision-making. Every student in our classrooms deserves to be seen and heard often. Let's take a look at how to do this.

This chapter addresses how to keep students at the center and build your community of learners by answering the following questions:

- [ ] **What does *student-centered* actually mean?**
- [ ] **How can I efficiently build relationships with students (even when I might have more than 200)?**
- [ ] **How can I connect with the kid who challenges me?**
- [ ] **How do I support students who are falling behind?**
- [ ] **How do I stand out to my students?**
- [ ] **How can I make sure my English learners feel a sense of belonging in my classroom?**
- [ ] **How can I make sure my students stay on task when I have a planned absence?**
- [ ] **How do I get students to follow classroom behavior expectations?**

What Does *Student-Centered* Actually Mean?

> Tell me, and I forget.
>
> Teach me, and I remember.
>
> Involve me, and I learn.
>
> —CLASSIC TEACHING PROVERB

A student-centered classroom is one in which the students are active participants in the learning process. This could look like students getting involved in the decision-making of a classroom with class votes—for example, students quickly voting on whether you ask an older grade or a younger grade to come in to see their projects. This could also look like students discussing and adding input about what they will be able to do for their final project of a unit. Student-centered learning also looks like students taking on leadership roles in the classroom with one another, like peer assessment, where students work together to give constructive feedback on one another's work before submitting it to the teacher.

Be gentle with yourself; a student-centered classroom can take time to build. In fact, John Hattie's synthesis of studies on the topic, detailed in his 2012 book, *Visible Learning for Teachers*, found that "teachers talk between 70 to 80 percent of class time, on average" (p. 72). However, this amount of teacher talk does not correspond with high engagement or even higher learning. Students' voices are heard more often in a student-centered classroom. In turn, students are more engaged in the learning, and learning happens on a deeper level. We have to be okay giving up a little control and letting the students take the reins throughout a lesson. In the classroom, we are teaching kids, not just content.

Helpful questions to ask yourself when working to create a student-centered classroom:

1. Do I allow student interest to drive how students will demonstrate a skill or concept?
2. Do students have an opportunity to choose how they will prove mastery of a concept?
3. Do students have ample opportunities to collaborate with one another?
4. Does my instruction include more student-led activities than direct instruction?
5. Does my content directly connect to the real world so it is relevant to students?
6. Do I allow opportunities for students to take part in the decision-making of our classroom?
7. Who does most of the talking in our classroom, the teacher or the students?

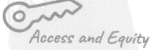

Access and Equity

All student voices should be heard equally. For those students who may be quieter or those who are learning English for the first time, ask for written input sometimes to make decisions about your instruction and classroom.

You may feel the impulse to . . .	Take a deep breath, and try this instead.
Make sure you have a 100 percent student-centered classroom from day one.	Be mindful that creating a student-centered classroom is a gradual process, and feel comfortable starting slowly.
Give the least amount of choice to a student who misbehaves or seems disengaged.	Consider giving these students the most amount of structured choice to help them feel a sense of ownership over the assignment and give it meaning. These students might not yet feel connected to the curriculum. Using their interests to meet a learning goal could increase engagement and meaning for these students.
Never have any direct instruction.	Understand that direct instruction can be purposeful in chunks (15 to 20 minutes) when a concept needs to be explained.

Ask Yourself:

- Who is doing most of the talking in my classroom? Me or my students?
- How can I adjust my lesson so I am doing less of the talking and my students are doing more?

Keep in Mind

When students ask you for a personal request or need, or there's something you have to do for them, write it down and let them see you doing it. It will validate their concerns and show you care. A sticky note works well.

STUDENTS

Notes

How Can I Efficiently Build Relationships With Students (Even When I Might Have More Than 200)?

The evidence is clear that we have to have a connection with our students. As Eric Karpinski (2021) writes, "Relationship researchers have shown that successful intimate relationships need about five positive-support interactions for each critical-challenging one. Tom Rath, senior scientist at Gallup, says we should target about 80 percent of our interaction time to be in positive areas—talking about successes and strengths—and only 20 percent to be in areas for improvement or difficulties" (p. 64). Teachers in upper grades may have more than 100 students, so there may not be enough time in the day or even the school year to form deep relationships with all of them. The key to building relationships when you have a large number of students is to do it efficiently. Yes, building relationships 1:1 is most definitely the more powerful way, but it is possible to efficiently build and quickly strengthen relationships with tiny decisions you make throughout the day, such as using a student's name when speaking to them. This does make a difference. There's only one of you and many of your students. It's important to take steps in more creative ways to save time in the long run, cut down on behavioral issues, cultivate a more positive classroom climate, increase learning in your classroom, and have happier students. When our students are happy, we are happy. Try these efficient ways to build relationships with multiple students at one time.

Strategies to efficiently build relationships with students:

- Hold morning meetings or circle meetings (once a week works well to start). Consider having students lead different parts of the meeting once they get the hang of it.
- Use students' names as often as possible when speaking to them.
- Celebrate and/or recognize birthdays.
- Do "get to know me" activities in class as icebreakers or team builders.
- Hold group conferences for books, essay check-ins, or other academic check-ins with three to five students at one time.
- When doing stations (meaning students rotate to different stations around the room to learn different concepts, often with a connecting theme), have one of the stations be a check-in with you to monitor progress and efficiently connect with students.
- When you can, attend school sports and extracurricular activities that your students participate in to see a nonacademic side of them (you might have 10 students on the basketball team).
- Use a note card to have students write down extracurricular interests so you can refer to it when needed. This can be done in the beginning of the school year.

● Create a "family board" or an area of the room dedicated to student pictures so students can see themselves and feel seen in the classroom (see Figure 2.1). Make sure you are equally showing all your students. Students who might not feel connected to the classroom, their peers, or the teacher might need to be on the family board the most. They shouldn't have to earn the right to be seen and heard.

Figure 2.1 This image is an example of a family board that can show pictures of students working, just being themselves, and having fun.

Source: Pariser and DeRoche, *Real Talk About Time Management* (2020).

STUDENTS

You may feel the impulse to . . .	Take a deep breath, and try this instead.
Hold a personal grudge toward students in your class who aren't doing well academically.	Know that these students need connection the most. Try thinking of at least one thing you genuinely like about these students.
Not take the time to learn about student interests and just focus on your academic curriculum.	Building relationships will actually help students become more interested in academics.
Hope that you happen to connect with every student throughout the year.	Use a checklist or set a goal to make contact with at least _____ students per week.
Not include on your family board pictures of students who misbehave in your classroom.	Know that a family board can help misbehaving students feel seen for who they are. Once they feel seen, they often will start to work harder in class, rather than striving for attention another way or shutting down. They will feel like they belong.

Ask Yourself:

How can I build relationships with my students efficiently and keep those relationships strong throughout the school year?

Notes

How Can I Connect With the Kid Who Challenges Me?

> Identify a student in the classroom who's a leader, even if the student leads in a negative way. Get to know that student and become friends—get the student on your side. Then the other kids will follow!
>
> —JACKIE HICKS, MIDDLE AND HIGH SCHOOL TEACHER

Most kids who challenge us are what we like to call "connection kids"; they have to like you to learn from you. Students whom teachers consider tougher are often used to getting disciplined and scolded, so they hesitate to really connect with adults and may test you in the beginning. It's important to have empathy. So if this is a student who has difficulty with every teacher, then take a different approach than the other teachers. It's first important to know *why* some students stay distant from us with defiance. Students who challenge us want to feel valued, seen, and heard.

Agency and Identity

A simple but effective strategy for the child who challenges you is to ask them to help you with something you can't figure out, such as a technology issue. Every person likes to be wanted. When they help you with something, they feel empowered, see that you trust them to help, and will become just a bit more connected to you.

Serena recalls a time in her fourth year teaching: Alan belted out songs in class whenever he felt like it, usually during silent reading time. He also walked around the room whenever he felt like it and picked and chose what he wanted to do in class. He single-handedly turned the classroom into a three-ring circus some days. As a teacher, Serena had to find a way to connect with him. Since classroom consequences weren't working, she decided to take a different approach. She noticed Alan had a lot of skateboarding stickers on his binder and started asking him things about skateboarding. Alan showed a picture of himself doing a trick called an ollie on his skateboard, and Serena asked if she could print it out to hang on the wall. Little by little Alan started to understand that his teacher cared about him and was curious about him as a human being as well as a student (who was severely underperforming). After that, Alan slowly but surely started doing work in class and stopped walking around the room.

Why do students misbehave? It's almost always one of these four reasons:

1 They want to feel empowered.
2 They feel inadequate. If a student feels academically inadequate, they most likely aren't getting the academic support they need in the classroom. Often, this leads to challenging behaviors. Academic support could look like small-group instruction, tutoring, 1:1 support with another adult, or peer tutoring.
3 They want to get even. For some reason they felt embarrassed in front of the class and need to "get even" to save face in front of their friends and classmates.
4 They want attention they aren't getting elsewhere or do not know how to get attention appropriately.

One of the most powerful mantras we can use when we have these types of students in our class is, don't take these misbehaviors personally. There is something deeper going on with these students, and it's helpful to give them space when needed. Don't make everything a fight. Tell them what you need them to do and then walk away. It's important that we listen to what the students who challenge us are saying. Often they will say things like, "That teacher just doesn't like me." What they are saying here is that the teacher isn't making an effort to connect with them. Also, it's important to remember that with kids, we have to give respect first before we get it.

It's a common misconception that with tougher students you have to show your authoritative power first, but that's completely opposite of what works in the long run. If we give our tougher students respect from the first moment we meet them, with our tone and words, we will often get respect back fairly quickly. If we do the opposite and try to overpower them or "show them who's boss," we will have a fight on our hands. Nobody wants that. With tougher students, being kind, confident, and consistent works well.

Most students who challenge us have been viewed by adults from a deficit-based lens rather than an asset lens. That means they have been told they aren't good at this or that, can't be quiet, constantly interrupt, or something else. Students hear these subtle messages from each teacher and internalize them, year after year. When we flip the script and ask about a student's interests and find out something they are good at (often outside of school), such as skateboarding, DJing, gaming, or putting on makeup, we are viewing them from an asset-based lens. They are being seen for something they are good at or like. This builds confidence in the child as they learn to trust us, and we can see them for who they really are. In turn, they will most likely start to work harder in our classroom because they will start to like us more.

It's important to remember that instead of pushing students out of our classroom when they challenge us, we want to form connections that help them engage with learning. Repeatedly pushing kids out of the classroom for behavior issues only puts them more at risk for falling behind academically. And there is clear evidence that over-disciplining children in the early years leads to higher incarceration rates, especially among children of color (Camera, 2021).

Keep in Mind

Challenging students want to be spoken to like everybody else. Be mindful of this when you say their names. Say them with the same tone as you would any other students'.

Agency and Identity

Some of the tougher students may have a more difficult time accessing or reaching your classroom expectations. This is where a behavior contract could be helpful for that little extra boost, and it allows students to take ownership of their improvement in your classroom. [See behavior contract section in Chapter 1, p. 31.]

Tip #1

Find at least one quality you like about students who challenge you. Refer to this list when needed to remind you of their strengths as students. Every student deserves a teacher who cares about them and believes in them.

Tip #2

Find at least one thing outside of school they are interested in. Ask about it. This shows them you care about them. Notice stickers they have on their binder, T-shirts they wear, or the types of drawings they make. Ask about these things to get to know the students better. These students want to be seen as human beings.

You may feel the impulse to . . .	Take a deep breath, and try this instead.
Hold a grudge against a student who challenges you.	Be optimistic about this student's behavior each day.
Scold this student publicly.	Always redirect the student quietly and privately, and praise publicly.
Kick a student out of the classroom or use other exclusionary discipline measures.	Take a deep breath, walk away, then find a time to have a follow-up conversation with the student.

Ask Yourself:

What is one nonacademic interest of a student who challenges me? Can I use this interest to connect them with my curriculum and classroom?

Notes

How Do I Support Students Who Are Falling Behind?

Students who have fallen behind in your classroom have probably lost a sense of having a voice in your classroom. This often results in behavior issues, as students want to feel seen and heard in some way. Keep in mind that students who have fallen behind academically may not know what they need to do to "catch up," and the failing spiral goes deeper and deeper, which potentially leads to behavior issues.

A method that often works is to have a conference with that student and have them leave with a sticky note of one to three tangible things they need to do and the date they need to have them done by. The sticky note could look something like this:

1 Finish vocab list from poetry unit by _____
2 Switch seats with Jania, starting _____
3 Come to after-school peer tutoring, starting _____

A written list can be very helpful, and students can check off assignments as they complete them to gain a sense of ownership and empowerment. Keeping it to three items doesn't overwhelm the student. Empower these students by pulling them aside during a non-class time and walking them through exactly what they need to do to catch up academically. If you can include the parents, even better. Also, make sure the students are aware of supports, like after-school tutoring, that may help them stay afloat. You'll probably notice behavior issues decreasing as they see you care and believe in them and they have direction again.

Sometimes students fall behind because they feel a sense of learned helplessness. This means that they are used to feeling lost or helpless and feel like there's no way out of it. Be sure all students can access your curriculum. This means English learners and students with Individualized Education Plans have support (purposeful seating chart, etc.) in place to succeed. This takes careful lesson planning and using data to inform instruction. For example, if you are writing a five-paragraph essay in class, you have made a list (perhaps just walking around the room and spot-checking) of students and how many paragraphs they have done. Perhaps you have a group of six students who have zero to three paragraphs done, so the next day you pull them into a small group led by an adult or even give them chart paper with instructions on how to get caught up while the others are working independently. Pulling kids into a small group allows you to work with them all in the same place as you circulate around the room. This is much easier than searching for the students who are behind as they work to hide themselves from the rest of the class.

Also, keep in mind that some students might not have academic role models at home who are encouraging them to do well in class. Many families rely on the teacher to take on this role for a number of reasons, including evening work hours or language barriers. Give ample opportunities for students to receive support in your class if they are falling behind.

Strategies for supporting students who are falling behind:

- Small-group catch-up: Pull students who are falling behind into a small group during independent work. This is an efficient way to help students because it's not 1:1, which takes way more time in the long run.
- One-day-a-week office hours: Consider holding office hours once a week on the same day after school or a weekly lunch tutoring session where students can receive extra help. Dedicating one day to it is more efficient than trying to schedule meetings with these students on different days of the week. To take the load off of you, you could ask for student tutors to volunteer for extra credit and help assist students during the session so you are not doing everything. This is especially helpful before a major project is due.
- Proactive mini lesson: Consider teaching all students a 20-minute mini lesson on how to speak to a teacher about falling behind and how to take steps to take action if they have fallen behind. We can't expect students to be able to do something we have not taught them, and this is a life skill they may not have been taught. Teaching this to students not only saves you frustration but sends a message that you care about students as human beings. Be careful not to take a condescending tone when teaching these lessons but rather a "you will need this skill in life" tone.

You may feel the impulse to . . .	Take a deep breath, and try this instead.
Just let students who didn't try hard enough fail.	Give students ample opportunities and support to succeed academically in your classroom. Students all learn in different ways.
Think, *It's their fault.*	Recognize your responsibility in helping students succeed academically and what supports you might have to put in place to help.
Get frustrated that students who have fallen behind have accepted the fact they have a failing grade.	Keep in mind that many students who often fall behind have developed a habit of learned helplessness. They think there's no hope and often don't know what they are missing. Giving students a written list or having them write a list of what they are missing can help remedy this issue.

Ask Yourself:

Do my students who are falling behind actually know what work they are missing or the support offered to them?

Notes

How Do I Stand Out to My Students?

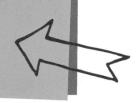

How do you want your students to remember you? There's a saying that students won't remember everything you taught them, but they will remember how you made them feel. There's a lot of truth in that statement.

Depending on the grade, by the time the students have you as a teacher, they may have had strict teachers, fun teachers, organized teachers, and funny teachers. But they haven't had one type of teacher just yet: you. There are different ways to stand out that students recognize and enjoy. When you stand out from other teachers, students will enjoy your class more and, in turn, will be more likely to be on task, engaged, and energized. That's way more fun for both you and your students. Students really like a lot of teachers, but in this section we are going to explore how you can not only be well-liked but really stand out to students.

What strategies can help you stand out to your students?

Tip #1 Adopt a warm demander approach.

In the words of Lisa Delpit (2013), "Warm demander teachers expect great things from their students, convince them of their own brilliance, and help them reach their potential in a disciplined, structured environment" (p. 77). Teachers with a warm demander approach expect a lot from each student but also support them in getting there. They expect students to take risks, and at the same time create a safe space for students to do so. They embrace student mistakes and see them as learning opportunities.

Tip #2 Give students power and a voice in your lessons.

Research has pointed to the fact that teachers talk 70 to 80 percent of the time. Further research suggests that number may be as high as 89 percent (Hattie, 2012). Unfortunately, a study that tracked middle and high school students found that engagement flagged the most when teachers were talking. So be the teacher who gives opportunities for students to talk. This could look like using class votes or polls in your lessons. Or it could look like, instead of calling on one or two people, asking all students to talk to their neighbors or groups about the answer to a question. When you give students time to discuss a question with their neighbors or groups, you'll get a higher response rate and more students will be talking. If students seem to freeze when you ask them to talk with a neighbor, ask them to write their answer first (quick jot), then discuss, then share out. This will get a much higher response rate. Your students should feel that it's their classroom, not just yours.

Another way to give students a voice is to consider giving them a feedback form (can be anonymous) asking their input and thoughts after each unit or midway through the year. You might elicit more thorough responses if you let them leave their names off the feedback forms and explain how you use their input. It's up to you, depending on your comfort level. Also, if you use a paper-and-pencil form as opposed to an electronic version, you'll most likely be able to tell by the handwriting which student filled out each form (even if they left their name off). The form could ask them simple questions about the unit so they can give you guidance about what is working well and what needs to be slightly adjusted for the next unit.

Sample questions to include on a student feedback form:

    a   How much do you feel like you learn in this class? (1–10)

    b   What did you like most about the last unit?

    c   What would you like to do more of in the next unit? Why?

    d   Do you feel that you get the academic support you need in this class? Why or why not?

    e   How challenging do you feel this class is? (1–10) Why?

    f   Do you get support from the people around you when needed? Why or why not?

    g   Is there anything Ms. Smith could do differently to help you succeed in this class? Please explain.

    h   Anything else? (You'd be surprised what your students may write here, and it's often a really cute thank-you or something along those lines.)

Tip #3

Be prepared with lessons daily. Be that adult they can rely on. Doing this alone shows how much you care about them and their education. This small difference will mean the world to the students—and they will notice.

Tip #4

Teach life skills as well as the content. In today's classrooms this looks like weaving life skills into the curriculum. Connect what they are learning to making them better human beings who are more prepared to succeed in the world. This could mean that you might be teaching older students not only how to write a résumé but also interview skills, and having them practice in class to meet the speaking and listening standards. In a younger classroom, this could mean when you read a book about two friends having a disagreement, you relate it back to their own life and teach conflict resolution and empathy skills so they can apply it to their own friendships.

Tip #5

Give small gifts during special holidays. Small and inexpensive gifts go a long way, especially when students do not feel like they had to earn them (there's a time and place for that); rather, you are giving them something because you care about them as human beings. Imagine how you'd feel as a student if a teacher brought in Halloween pencils and a piece of candy for each student and had these gifts on the students' desks when they walked in the week of Halloween? This shows you unconditionally care about each and every student. Something very small can go a long way toward building a strong connection with students.

Tip #6

Another strategy that goes a long way is being mindful that you **do not favor some students over others**. It's easy to do this and not realize it, so check in with yourself regularly. Is there a student you always ask to do the fun errands? Perhaps mix up who you send. All your students want and deserve to feel heard and seen. If you have a student or two who seem to be driving you bonkers (and you probably will), try making a list of those students' strengths and focus on those, and then continue to show up as their teacher. They will come around. Allowing all your students to feel like you respect them equally will help you stand out to your students. Keep in mind that your students come from different cultures, have different backgrounds, and have different personality traits. Some students may not feel comfortable speaking openly with teachers and may just want to listen and complete work quietly, while some may feel comfortable opening up to you as they do other teachers. It's important to remember that as teachers the most important thing we can do with students to stand out is care about them with our actions as well as our words.

Tip #7

Invite guest speakers (virtual or in person) into the classroom to bring the learning to life. Students will remember this. Bringing in a guest speaker can

- show your students you care about their learning,
- bring the curriculum to life,
- show the students you trust them,
- connect the lessons to the real world, and
- help students practice speaking and listening skills.

At the end, always save time for a Q and A and let the students interact with the speaker.

You may want to do a mini lesson to prep students on how to address the speaker and how to thank them, greet them, and ask questions.

Examples of guest speakers who could bring the curriculum to life:

- Bring in an attorney (or two) when you are teaching a debate unit. Often, organizations are looking for ways to get involved with schools; they just don't have a contact to do so.
- Ask a local poet to come in and share their work and story during a unit where students are learning to write poetry.
- Invite in or video-conference with a family member of a Holocaust survivor when you are reading literature on that subject.

Keep in Mind

Having students create questions beforehand to ask the guest speaker leads to a richer Q and A. Of course, impromptu questions are always welcome as well.

Great Resources

- Blog post: Alexander, M. (2016, April 13). The warm demander: An equity approach. *Edutopia*. https://www.edutopia.org/blog/warm-demander-equity-approach-matt-alexander

- Chart: Hammond, Z. (2015). "Warm demander chart." In *Culturally responsive teaching and the brain* (p. 99). Corwin. https://bit.ly/3ILlz1L

You may feel the impulse to . . .	Take a deep breath, and try this instead.
Just not like all your students.	Be mindful of all your students' strengths. Make a list of their strengths to help you remember. Give other students chances to shine. Students can tell when a teacher likes them or not. It's your job to like every student and speak to them in the same tone.
Get frustrated or shame the class if nobody is answering a question.	Have the students do a quick jot and talk to a neighbor, *then* ask the students to share out. You should get a higher response rate.

Ask Yourself:

What makes me stand out from every other teacher this student has had throughout their life?

Notes

How Can I Make Sure My English Learners Feel a Sense of Belonging in My Classroom?

> While EL is used by the federal government and most states to describe students who are exposed to a language in addition to English, some argue that the term "English Learner" focuses more on students' deficits of learning a language while ignoring the strength of their home language.
>
> —SYDNEY SNYDER AND DIANE STAEHR FENNER, *CULTURALLY RESPONSIVE TEACHING FOR MULTILINGUAL LEARNERS* (2021, P. 2)

At the time of this writing, there is a shift in education in how students who are learning English as a new language are referred to. For many years, schools and teachers have referred to these students as ELs (English learners) or ELLs (English language learners), but in an effort to honor students' first languages as well as the wealth of language experiences, culture, and wider world view they bring into our classrooms, the term "emerging bilingual" students has been adopted by many schools across the United States (Garcia, 2021). Many doors can open for these students as they are becoming fully bilingual, so we must nurture their development in this process; confidence is often what they need most of all. The issue is, students learning English will often be shy or even embarrassed in our classes at first. Every student deserves to feel like they belong to—like they are an integral part of—a learning community in order to thrive.

First, and most important, we need to view these students from a strengths-based model, meaning we recognize the assets of these students—the skills and knowledge they bring into our classrooms. Often, these assets are found outside of our classrooms, perhaps in a different content area, on the sports field, in an art room, or in hobbies they enjoy. Students who are EL learners, while often timid in our classrooms (especially if it's an English language arts class), have rich experiences and knowledge to share but can often feel a bit shy in an academic setting that is rich with language.

It's up to us to make sure emerging bilingual learners feel like they belong socially and academically to our classrooms, and this can take a bit of time. Give opportunities for EL students to show their strengths in your classroom. This could look like José bringing a picture of himself riding his moped for you to hang near your desk or in a dedicated area of the room. Here are other strategies that can help your EL learners feel a sense of belonging in your classroom:

1   You can create a sense of belonging by making sure the books in your classroom library represent a variety of cultures, especially those of the emerging bilingual students.

2   Include EL students in all class activities. If it's an activity where a student may struggle, pair them with another student who can help them succeed, to collaborate and gain confidence. If that student speaks the EL student's native language, even better!

3   Use small bits of the native language of your EL learner in simple ways to help them feel included. This can look like simply writing "Hola" in addition to "Good morning" on the board. The more languages that are included in tiny pieces, the better. Label items around your classroom in EL learners' native language, too.

4   Use images throughout your lesson to provide visual cues to ELs. This can help other students in the room, too, who might need more support.

5   In the beginning of the school year, ask them what their strengths, passions, and hobbies are. This can be a writing exercise with the entire class, or they can draw pictures or point to images online.

6   Notice when you see the student succeed in ways other than just in your classroom. Let them know! This will help build a sense of confidence in the student.

7   Urge these students to connect to the school outside of your classroom through a sport or extracurricular activity.

Great Resource

Book: Snyder, S., & Fenner, D. (2021). *Culturally responsive teaching for multilingual learners: A toolkit for equity.* Corwin.

You may feel the impulse to . . .	Take a deep breath, and try this instead.
Seat all your EL students at the same table or area so you can always help them together.	See the seating chart section in Chapter 1. It's important that your EL students feel as much a part of your classroom as your other students. They may also need the academic/language/writing collaboration opportunities with their classmates.
Assume EL students bring less academically to the table than your general education students do.	Keep in mind that your EL students may have richer funds of knowledge than your general education students but may be less comfortable opening up. Sit them next to a kind student they can feel comfortable with. If that student speaks their native language as well, even better.

Ask Yourself:

Have I noticed a strength in each of my EL students and let them know I see it?

Notes

How Can I Make Sure My Students Stay on Task When I Have a Planned Absence?

> Some of my former students remember four years ago when I flew to Virginia to be in a friend's wedding. They remember this because I told them about how she and I became friends and why it was important that I went. I told them a funny story about an incident that happened at the wedding when I returned. They enjoyed being a part of my life for a second. If I had not had this conversation, I would have been just another teacher who missed another day. A conversation such as this will not only empower the students with knowledge but also show the students you value their learning and their trust.
>
> —MIDDLE SCHOOL TEACHER

First, don't miss too many days. Students' worlds revolve around themselves and they are not adults just yet. So they may not grasp the concept that life does happen outside of school—people get married, kids have appointments, and some days you may just not be there. However, missing too many days in the classroom can be interpreted by a student as meaning you don't care—and we know that isn't the case.

The truth is that there are going to be a few days when we are going to have planned absences, and these days can be an opportunity to empower your students. To do this, if possible go over the lesson plan in detail with your class at the end of the period the day before you will be absent. Even show them the letter you are writing to the substitute teacher. Ask if they have any questions. Why do this? While you're gone, your students will understand exactly what to do, they'll feel confident, and the sub will be happy. It's a win-win.

Here's a script for a conversation to have with your classroom at the end of class the day before your absence:

"Students, I want to speak with you seriously for five minutes, and I need your attention. My best friend is getting married this Saturday, and the wedding is in Virginia. I have been invited to the wedding and have to take a flight tomorrow morning. Unfortunately, I will not be here tomorrow but will be back on Monday. Now, let's talk about how we respect a guest teacher. What types of behaviors do I expect when a guest is in the room?"

You may get some questions here about the actual event or reason for your absence, and that's all right. Personalize it as much as feels comfortable. Show them you are human, not just a teacher "ditching out" on them. They will end up appreciating you more for this.

You can chart these behaviors or write them somewhere so students can see them the next day.

* Tip #1

Have directions for students already written out so the substitute can just project them as they take attendance.

* Tip #2

Have a seating chart ready for the substitute.

* Tip #3

Let the substitute know where the bathroom is and how to open it if it is locked. (This seems obvious, but it doesn't always happen.)

* Tip #4

Perhaps list one or two names of students the substitute can ask for any needed assistance.

You may feel the impulse to . . .	Take a deep breath, and try this instead.
Assume your class is going to be out of control when you are not there.	Take the steps above to set students up for success. There's nothing like having a conversation with a substitute praising a class's behavior after you have been gone for a day.
Not let your class know in advance when you will have a planned absence.	Understand that letting your class know when you will not be there gives them a sense of control over the situation.

Ask Yourself:

How can I best set my students up for success when I know I'm going to be absent, and make sure the learning continues?

Notes

How Do I Get Students to Follow Classroom Behavior Expectations?

An excellent way for you to create an inclusive environment is to ask questions as you make and practice the classroom expectations.

When developing your classroom expectations, ask students to think about the following:

1. How will this behavior expectation affect all students in the classroom?
2. Why should students exhibit this behavior?
3. Does this expectation encourage everyone to be their best self?

Have students encourage one another to meet and exceed their class behavior and academic goals. This is where seating students in groups of four to five can help with student motivation to keep one another focused and working.

An option more teachers are trying is to have all your students' voices involved in creating your classroom expectations. Your role as a teacher is to prompt them with questions that will help them consider multiple perspectives; this will ensure all students are included, seen, and heard. The earlier a classroom expectation is established, the better. Day two of a school year is an optimal time to go over expectations. Day one can be saved for a fun icebreaker or team-building activity.

Broader expectations work well so more expectations can be covered and still kept to a list of four to six. They should also be stated in the positive. For example:

Effective classroom expectation: Respect all classmates and adults with words and actions.
Not as effective: No hitting.

Effective classroom expectation: Respect all classroom materials.
Not as effective: No drawing on desks.

Here is an example of a set of classroom expectations:

1. Respect all classmates, adults, and materials.
2. Participate.
3. Respect personal space of others.
4. Use appropriate language.
5. Respect each other's thoughts, opinions, and ideas.

Tip #1

Allow student voice in creating behavior expectations so students feel a sense of ownership of classroom expectations and can support one another in following them.

How Do I Get Students to Follow Classroom Behavior Expectations?

55

Tip #2

Have students take pictures of themselves showing how to follow and not follow the expectations. This creates student ownership of the expectations and also adds a layer of fun to it.

Tip #3

Have only a handful of behavior expectations (four to six) that are broad enough to cover many issues that may arise.

You may feel the impulse to . . .	Take a deep breath, and try this instead.
Tell the students how to follow the expectations.	Explain the reason behind the expectation at the beginning of the school year and give examples as well as non-examples of what each expectation looks like. Have fun with it. For instance, as non-examples, pretend to be a student talking back to a teacher, roll your eyes, or demonstrate some other behavior that would normally not be acceptable. Then demonstrate the alternative, positive example. This gets the students thinking about how and why the expectations impact them and their peers.
Have a different set of expectations for each period.	This will most likely overwhelm you. It's best to have the same four to six expectations for each classroom.
Motivate students by offering free time.	While this sounds like a good idea, it can quickly turn to chaos. Students love structure. You can still give them autonomy by giving them choices. The key is to expect that they have to engage in one of the choices you offer.
Not have the students create rationale for the expectations.	The teacher identifies the expectation; the students create the steps and rationale. This promotes ownership and agency.
Wait until the class needs behavior expectations before implementing them.	Remember that introducing behavior expectations early sets students up for success, instead of leaving them unclear about what they can and can't do.

Ask Yourself:

What are some methods to have my students hold their peers accountable for their behavior?

Recap: Try This Tomorrow

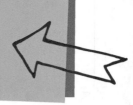

Each of these strategies takes little prep and can help guide you to the answers for keeping students at the center.

- When making your lessons, try to have the students doing about 60 to 70 percent of the talking. It's helpful, as it increases as the week progresses. It will take some work, but you can get there!
- Take pictures of your students working or having fun inside and outside of your classroom to later post in a designated spot, like a family board, in your classroom.
- Listen to what our "tough kids" are saying. Often they will say things like, "That teacher just doesn't like me." What they are saying here is that the teacher isn't making an effort to connect with them.
- Pull students who are falling behind into a small group during independent work. This is an efficient way to help students because it's not 1:1, which takes way more time. This can be done by you or a co-teacher.
- Hold a belief that every student wants to and can learn.
- Use class votes or polls in your lesson to offer students more of a voice.
- If you have English language learners in your classroom, seat them next to a kind non-EL student they can feel comfortable with. If that student speaks their native language as well, even better.
- To empower your students when you have a planned absence, go over the lesson plan with them in detail the day before. Ask if they have any questions.

Notes

STUDENTS

chapter THREE

HOW CAN I DESIGN EFFECTIVE, FUN, AND ENGAGING LEARNING FOR STUDENTS?

Imagine This

Your students love working collaboratively, are sitting in heterogeneous groups set up for success, and are able to stay on task while also staying highly engaged. You become less of a sage on the stage and more of a facilitator, circling the classroom. Your lessons are everything students want: Students get to frequently work together, and your lessons use a plethora of visuals and technology to maximize the learning. Your students know how the lessons connect to the real world. You know students are visual creatures by nature, and you use this to enhance your lessons. You also add movement into the lessons because you know kids need to move and it also helps the learning. Your lessons also have student choice, as you know this increases engagement. Your students are hooked on what you are teaching and learning engaging and rigorous content. You are able to make the learning relevant and meaningful for your students.

Your students have opportunities to create projects throughout the school year that they can be proud of and that highlight their critical thinking and creative ability based on what they learned in your classroom. Your lessons purposefully mix up learning and engagement styles to reach all learners.

You understand how to use your effective lesson plans to increase engagement. You have a system (perhaps with your co-teacher) where you carve out weekly time to create daily lesson plans a week ahead of time and are on the same page with your co-teacher about what the students will be learning that day. You are always a step or two ahead of your students.

If a student finishes their work early, they know exactly what to do and do not show off-task, distracting behavior. If a student falls behind in learning a concept, you know how to differentiate instruction to catch that student up, or a group of students. It's all a dance you've been perfecting.

Most days, you do a bit of direct instruction, perhaps 15 to 20 minutes, as you know many students learn best with collaborative learning strategies. You know learning is a social activity.

As you are teaching, you know how to comfortably add humor and a bit of your own unique personality to the lesson. Your students know you care about them just as much as you care about the content. Your students have a deep respect for you as a teacher and as a human being. This can be your reality.

The backbone of any thriving classroom is a teacher's skill and motivation to design effective, fun, and engaging learning for all students. Engagement simply means students are really into a lesson. This can look like students laughing and smiling or like students thinking very critically and working diligently on something. This takes a lot of work behind the scenes, but it's worth it. In addition to being engaged and having fun, students actually learn more during this type of teaching than during traditional direct instruction. Every student deserves this type of education. Not only does designing these kinds of lessons benefit student learning, but it also helps you have more fun and enjoyment while teaching. Designing effective, fun, and engaging lessons, simply put, is our job. This comes with practice, patience, creativity, and collaboration. A teacher who becomes highly skilled at developing lessons will always succeed and have more engaged students.

In this chapter about designing effective, fun, and engaging learning for students, the following questions will be addressed:

- ☐ **What do students really want in a lesson?**
- ☐ **What are some often overlooked pieces of lesson planning?**
- ☐ **How do I make my lesson plans relevant, rigorous, and fun all at the same time?**
- ☐ **How do I use technology effectively in my lessons to maximize learning?**
- ☐ **How do I get ahead with planning, with so many other tasks to do?**
- ☐ **How do I keep students on task with group work?**
- ☐ **What if a student finishes their work early?**
- ☐ **What are some learning activities that are more engaging, fun, and collaborative than direct instruction?**

What Do Students Really Want in a Lesson?

> Engaging students not only helps them love to learn, but it helps us love to teach. We all entered this profession excited to spark an interest of learning, to see that light bulb pop with excitement over a student's head. This can only happen if we put effort into engaging the students before us.
>
> —HEATHER WOLPERT-GAWRON,
> *JUST ASK US: KIDS SPEAK OUT ON ENGAGEMENT* (2018, P. 4)

A video titled "Does Engagement Equal Fun?" from *Just Ask Us* (Wolpert-Gawron, 2018)

https://players
.brightcove
.net/268012963001/
rJenILPQx_default/
index.html?videoId
=5485870986001

In 2018, author Heather Wolpert-Gawron debunked a common misconception that engagement doesn't always equal fun—and that's demonstrated in her book *Just Ask Us: Kids Speak Out on Engagement*. Wolpert-Gawron surveyed more than 1,000 K–12 students nationwide and asked them what they specifically want in a lesson, what engages them. Interestingly, what the students reported matched up with what the data suggest is beneficial to student engagement and teacher satisfaction.

Students reported:

1. Let us work together.
2. Make learning more visual and utilize technology.
3. Connect what we learn to the real world.
4. Let us move around.
5. Give us choices.
6. Show us you're human, too.
7. Help us create something with what we've learned.
8. Teach us something in a new way.
9. Mix things up.

What does this actually mean? Let's break it down a bit more.

What Students Reported Really Wanting in a Lesson	What This Actually Looks Like in Your Classroom
Let us work together.	Group work, partner work, friendly competition in class or units; having a class earn badges or "level up" together (e.g., a class thermometer to keep track of progress); having students contribute to "shared" documents as much as possible to build a sense of community
Make learning more visual and utilize technology.	Photos or cartoons to explain a concept, visuals to explain a concept

What Students Reported Really Wanting in a Lesson	What This Actually Looks Like in Your Classroom
Connect what we learn to the real world.	Project-based learning, authentic audiences for projects (other grades in a school, community members, etc.)
Let us move around.	Class debates, stations, carousel learning, movement activities, providing unique seats where students can move their bodies a bit while they work
Give us choices.	Structured choice, ability-tiered student choice where students choose the tier comfortable to them, allowing students to choose how they would like to do a project, giving students choice on project topics
Show us you're human, too.	Using humor in lessons, sharing certain elements of your life, being honest if you mess up
Help us create something with what we've learned.	Incorporating creation in every unit (drawings, gadgets, inventions, trifolds, storybooks)
Teach us something in a new way.	Teaching in ways other than direct instruction
Mix things up.	Use different multiple intelligences in a lesson, fun experiments, acting-out skits, comedy sketches to illustrate a concept

Keep in Mind

Know that students want to know who you are as a human being.
Don't be afraid to smile and laugh sometimes while you are teaching.
They'll be more connected to both the content *and* you.

Great Resources

- Blog post: Wolpert-Gawron, H. (2015, February 24). Kids speak out on student engagement. *Edutopia.* https://www.edutopia.org/blog/student-engagement-stories-heather-wolpert-gawron

- Book: Wolpert-Gawron, H. (2018). *Just ask us: Kids speak out on engagement.* Corwin.

You may feel the impulse to . . .	Take a deep breath, and try this instead.
Arrange the desks in rows because your students won't stop talking.	Perhaps try seating them in pairs of two, facing you. Then you can work your way back to groups but they can still collaborate a bit in a highly structured setting.
Seat groups homogeneously (same ability level) as their permanent seats.	Try heterogeneous groups so all groups are set up for success. It's powerful to pull homogeneous groups together for a few minutes for small-group instruction to reteach a lesson or revisit a concept if needed.
Do direct instruction most of a period because you have so much to teach and can cover a concept quicker that way.	Know that although direct instruction may be a faster way to "cover" a concept, students most likely won't retain information this way. So it will actually take more time in the long run.

Ask Yourself:

When creating your lessons, think: *Would I want to learn a concept this way? If not, how can I add one of the helpful tips above to a lesson?*

Notes

What Are Some Often Overlooked Pieces of Lesson Planning?

> *If only I had taken a little more time to plan for my instruction, maybe I would not have had such a chaotic, stressful day. I realized why the need to plan was so critical. My students were more engaged, and I was less stressed. I felt energized at the end of the day. I was hooked. From that day forward, taking the time to plan my lessons gave me freedom and time to help students that needed more attention.*
>
> —VICTORIA LENTFER

So why do you need a lesson plan? Here are a few key reasons why having a lesson plan helps:

- You will be doing a million and one things during class. A lesson plan will keep you on track. It will also prevent you from forgetting a crucial part of a lesson.
- There are multiple components to an effective lesson plan, and things are often overlooked when teaching without one. Referring to your lesson plan while you are teaching will ensure you remember every part.
- You are driving the instruction and pace of the class, instead of the class driving your pace.
- As you are making your lesson plan, you can proactively accommodate the additional needs of your students with Individualized Education Plans (IEPs) and English learners (ELs) before they fall behind and become apathetic or develop other behavioral issues.
- An effective lesson plan helps you, the teacher, think deeply about the flow of the unit and the needs of the students, and how to engage them. This work should be done behind the scenes.

However, there are a few pieces of a lesson plan that are often overlooked. Here we dig into three components—activating prior knowledge, sufficient scaffolding, and movement—that can make a huge positive impact in your lessons. (Figure 3.1 shows an example of a lesson that incorporates these three components.)

Activating Prior Knowledge, or Including an Engaging Anticipatory Set at the Start of a Lesson

Looks like: Having the students respond to a five-minute prompt before you start, to link the day's learning to the prior day or link what you are teaching to what they already know from their lives, or both; showing a quick two- to three-minute clip relating to something you are about to teach and asking a question

Example: Question: "Remember what you learned yesterday about the periodic table of elements. Now, why do you think each element also has an atomic number listed with it, and what do you think is its purpose?" (Then you would go into a lesson on atomic numbers for that day.)

Purpose: You are building on what students already know or what they think, or getting them hooked on what you are about to teach, leading to increased student engagement as you launch into the lesson.

Sufficient Scaffolding

Looks like: Guided instruction

Example: Teacher is practicing on a document camera *with* the students before they practice on their own; students are practicing *with* each other before they practice on their own; students are practicing *with* each other or a teacher in small groups before they practice on their own.

Purpose: Guided instruction helps the teacher assess how well the students understand the material before they are asked to do it independently. It also gives the students opportunities to fix mistakes and gaps in knowledge with the teacher or each other before they practice on their own.

Movement

Looks like: Any time a student is on their feet, moving their body, or doing anything other than sitting still the entire period

Examples: Getting up to work in partners around the room, station learning, moving to a small group, carousel activities, gallery walks, quick movement breaks to transition (e.g., from the reading portion of the lesson to the writing portion), using hand or body motions to learn concepts or vocabulary words, sorting activities

Purpose: Many of our students are kinesthetic learners, and movement will help accentuate the learning. Also, students are asked to sit through hours a day of learning. Without movement, many students will quickly become disengaged, even though they may seem like they are engaged.

Great Resources

- Blog post: Ferlazzo, L. (2020, July 24). Eight ways to use movement in teaching and learning. *EdWeek*. https://www.edweek.org/teaching-learning/opinion-eight-ways-to-use-movement-in-teaching-learning/2020/07

- Blog post: Gillyard, A. (2016, November 1). 3 ways lesson plans flop—and how to recover. *Edutopia*. https://www.edutopia.org/blog/3-ways-lesson-plans-flop-how-to-recover-anne-gillyard

- Blog post: Gonzalez, J. (2014, September 6). Know your terms: Anticipatory set. *Cult of Pedagogy*. https://www.cultofpedagogy.com/anticipatory-set/

Tip #1

Use a timer while teaching each part of a lesson plan (or have a co-teacher time you) to keep yourself on pace while teaching based on the lesson plan. Keeping up the pace keeps engagement going!

Tip #2

Write what you want the students to learn, then begin to sharpen it by writing it as specifically as possible. Creating learning targets will provide clarity when you make your lessons.

Tip #3

Write the objective on the board and refer to it while teaching so students know the purpose of your lesson.

Tip #4

Remember to include at least 15 minutes or more of guided practice daily. This is when the learning happens, and it's also the part most often overlooked.

You may feel the impulse to . . .	Take a deep breath, and try this instead.
Plow through the lesson to "get through the material," without guided instruction.	Remember that if you go right from teaching a concept to independent practice, many students may get lost, especially with a more difficult concept.
Leave out movement because your students might not want to get up and move.	Remember that any type of movement helps learning and sometimes students want to take the path of least resistance, especially in the high school years.
Jump right into learning without activating prior knowledge because you have so much to teach.	Remember that students need to see how lessons build on each other and also how a lesson can connect to the world around them. If you are really short on time, simply have them talk to a partner quickly about the question that activates prior knowledge, rather than having them write it down.

Ask Yourself:

If I had a lesson that flopped, did I forget one of these three pieces?

Figure 3.1. Example of a Lesson That Includes the 3 Often Overlooked Pieces (Bolded Text)

Lesson objective: Given a collection of poems, students will analyze personification on a graphic organizer by explaining, illustrating, and adding movement to understand personification in poems.

5 minutes	**Watch the two-minute clips from *Beauty and the Beast* that include many examples of personification. Ask students to jot down responses: What did you notice the objects doing during the movie that they can't do in real life? Example answers: dancing teacups, laughing water. Share responses with a neighbor, then with the class.**	Anticipatory set
5 minutes	Model: Project a model poem with personification using a document camera. Show explanations and illustrations already completed next to specific lines in the poem (to save time) and why it is personification (using metacognition or "thinking aloud" as students listen to you think). As a class, construct a definition for personification and compare it with a definition that can be found online.	
15 to 20 minutes	Guided instruction: After reading a second poem with the class at their seats, have students repeat lines after you as you read. **Then have table groups of students work together to explain in writing which lines of the poem contain personification and why** (just as you did for the model poem). **Next, have groups collectively come up with a hand or body motion to help them remember what each term means.**	Scaffolding Movement
10 minutes	Independent: Have individual students start to work independently to complete a graphic organizer to analyze a third poem with the same illustrations and explanations they did for the first two poems. They can finish at home if needed.	
5 minutes	Closure: Ask students to write down three other examples of personification on an exit slip to assess understanding of your teaching. Have students talk with a partner and share their learning with the class.	

Source: Adapted from *Real Talk About Time Management* (Pariser & DeRoche, 2020).

How Do I Make My Lesson Plans Relevant, Rigorous, and Fun All at the Same Time?

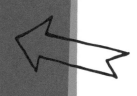

What do relevant lessons look like in the classroom? Relevant lessons connect to the world around the students. Students see direct meaning in why they are learning a concept and understand how the concepts or unit will help them with their need to make sense of the world. In the chart on the next page, you'll see examples of how the teacher made the lessons relevant to the students by providing different experiences. These experiences include providing an authentic audience using technology for a writing assignment, taking students on a field trip so they can see and learn more about the endangered species they are studying, and inviting guest speakers into the classroom to bring their legal system unit to life.

What do rigorous lessons look like in a classroom? Rigorous means that students are thinking critically about the content. This means they are thinking at a higher level than recognizing and recalling facts. Instead they are explaining concepts, applying what they know to analyze or evaluate, or even creating something. Most likely this means that students are bouncing ideas off of each other, scratching their heads, and deeply engaging in the work—rather than just completing a worksheet. In the chart on the next page, you'll see how the teacher created rigorous lessons, including analyzing the purposes of different parts of an introductory paragraph, having students create their own research questions to guide their exploration, and asking students not only to learn about the different parts of a courtroom and how they function but to evaluate the system.

What does fun instruction mean and look like in a classroom? Fun instruction basically means students look forward to doing it. Fun takes a bit of creativity and thinking outside the box. It's when teachers think: *What's a creative way the students could learn this concept?* They're excited to come to class and are eager to participate and take risks in the classroom. Let's face it: students have so much to learn in their K–12 journey. Why not make most of it fun and something they actually want to do? In the chart below, you'll see examples of how a teacher made learning fun in different ways. One of the methods was asking students to color-code the different parts of an introductory paragraph instead of simply labeling in pencil. This also helps visual learners. Additionally, the teacher not only provided opportunities for students to collaborate together but also gave structured choice in working on a topic based on student interest. Also, the teacher showed a short clip of an engaging and dramatic television show to contextualize the concepts the students would be learning that day. There are different levels of fun, too. Sometimes fun can simply be using the nice art supplies, and sometimes it can be transforming the entire classroom into a live game show where students are practicing concepts for the upcoming assessment.

INSTRUCTION

	Examples of How to Make Curriculum *Rigorous*	Examples of How to Make Curriculum *Fun*	Examples of How to Make Curriculum *Relevant*
Learning how to write a persuasive essay in an English classroom	Showing students an example of an introductory paragraph in an essay and having them point out and explain the parts and analyze their purposes, rather than giving the parts first in direct instruction	Having students color-code the different parts of an introductory paragraph with highlighters in addition to labeling	Writing a persuasive essay in an email to a homeless shelter in an effort to give them ideas for how to help the local population of unhoused people as cold weather approaches
Learning about endangered species in a science classroom	Having students create their own research questions before starting their research to find answers about their endangered species	Letting students work together and choose their own species to research from a list you have created	Taking students on a field trip to the zoo, where they can see the endangered species firsthand and the efforts the world is making to protect this species
Learning about the legal system in our society in a history classroom	Asking students to evaluate how a courtroom works and how it can be improved and why	Showing different clips (two to three minutes) of *Law and Order* before you start the lesson each day to provide a visual of the part of the courtroom you are learning about that day	Inviting attorneys into the classroom to talk about the courtroom and answer questions from the students

You may feel the impulse to . . .	Take a deep breath, and try this instead.
"Tread water" with lesson planning and be only one or two days ahead with it because of having too much to do.	Try creating a four- to six-week project from start to finish to get your class engaged and learning. This is time you carve out for yourself and put everything else aside.
Do assignments just to get through the curriculum.	Spend time planning curriculum that connects directly with the real world.
"Threaten" students with failure if they do not complete a project or assignment.	Add a competitive edge to the projects to add some fun and an extra layer of engagement.
Have students complete a project and then turn it in only for a grade.	Invite parents, other classes (younger or older), and other teachers to see presentations to add an authentic audience.

Ask Yourself:

Would I want to do the lessons I create? (If the answer is no, try something different.)

Answers to Your Biggest Questions About Creating a Dynamic Classroom

How Do I Use Technology Effectively in My Lessons to Maximize Learning?

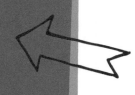

> *The technology we have today is a game changer because it can *help* create magic in the classroom—however, only to the extent that schools and teachers are prepared and engaged.*
>
> —CATLIN R. TUCKER, TIFFANY WYCOFF, AND JASON T. GREEN,
> *BLENDED LEARNING IN ACTION* (2017, P. 4)

Technology can be a blessing and a curse, as many of us learned during the 2020–2021 school year when we had to scramble into virtual learning mode. However, now we can apply some of what we learned in that crisis mode to our everyday practice. For example, we know that technology can rarely be a substitute for powerful in-person teaching, but it can be a wonderful complement. We also now know that a student sitting in front of a computer, staring at the screen, is not always fully engaged in the learning.

Learning should still be a social activity with technology use. Be sure to add purposeful collaboration opportunities on the days you implement technology in your lessons. Often with technology we see a lack of collaboration and conversation among students. Remember to keep your EL students in mind when incorporating technology into your lessons; they should not be "hiding" behind a computer screen all period.

Know when technology actually enhances learning—and keep in mind that sometimes a pen and paper are just faster. Always have a backup plan if your lesson relies solely on technology, in case the technology does not work that day. The Internet could be out, the computers might not have been charged, or some other unexpected glitch could make technology unreliable.

Ask a few students to be "helpers" the day you use technology, to assist you with minor technological glitches. Choose students who are naturally good with technology. If you have a second adult in the room, you could also ask them for help. You will want to make sure you aren't tied down by too many minor glitches that take you away from teaching a lesson.

Helpful Ways Technology Can Enhance a Lesson

How to Enhance a Lesson With Technology	What That Looks Like in a Classroom
Provide an authentic audience for students.	Students could write emails to local community members about issues in the community for a letter-writing unit. Or students could email community members with a solution to a societal problem after a research unit.

How Do I Use Technology Effectively in My Lessons to Maximize Learning?

69

INSTRUCTION

How to Enhance a Lesson With Technology	What That Looks Like in a Classroom
Incorporate technology in station learning.	Technology can act as the teacher for one station, as students could be asked to watch a short video together on a laptop and then do a reflection or answer questions.
Add a high amount of visual stimulation to a lesson.	Use photos or short videos in a lesson to enhance a concept or help make it more concrete.
Create shared documents with the class to foster a sense of community.	Use Padlet or Google Drive to create one class document of their hypothesis about what might happen in an experiment.
Use instant polls in lessons.	Adding student polls in lessons can dramatically increase engagement in a lesson.
Give feedback in real time.	Live documents, such as Google Slides or Google Docs, can be shared with the teacher as students are working. The teacher can check in at any time and add feedback as students are working.

You may feel the impulse to . . .	Take a deep breath, and try this instead.
Stray away from technology in fear that it might not work.	Find out what student is gifted with technology in your classroom so you can ask for help if needed.
Use technology for an entire class period.	Know that even when students are using technology, there should be an aspect of collaboration. This can mean they stop their technology projects and simply show each other what they are doing for a few minutes to assess each other. This helps build a community of learners.

Ask Yourself:

Are the students still getting a chance to stop and collaborate on progress and give feedback to each other on assignments while using technology?

Notes

_____

_____

_____

_____

_____

_____

_____

_____

_____

_____

_____

_____

How Do I Get Ahead With Planning, With So Many Other Tasks to Do?

> One thing that helped me a lot is being prepared: lesson plans, planning, resources. Popularity comes from having your learners intrigued, which comes from being prepared and going the extra mile, especially as a new teacher.
>
> —MR. SAWYERS

The most effective thing you can do is carve out weekly planning time in your schedule and stay one week ahead of daily planning, after you have roughly sketched out a unit. If you have a co-teacher, invite them into the process of planning.

Honor that planning time, turn off phones, and close the door. Consider putting your phone out of sight, even if you have it on silent or off, so it doesn't take your attention away from the task at hand.

Getting ahead with lesson planning allows you to be more present when you are teaching. As you are planning, be sure to make accommodations and modifications for students with IEPs and GATE (Gifted and Talented Education) students. When we get ahead with planning, we can proactively support these learners more effectively. When we are a week ahead with planning (which is an optimal spot), we can make meaningful and relevant lesson plans rather than scrambling to fill time.

Keep in Mind

Nothing is more important than creating strong lesson plans to decrease student behavioral issues, increase engagement, and decrease stress in your life.

If there is one constant, it is that there will *always* be something other than lesson planning that needs to be done during this time. For other tasks that might pop into your head as you are planning, use a sticky note to write down the task so you don't forget it and can address it later. This will help you stay focused so you can continue to plan with your entire mind. You want to keep the momentum going, and forming the healthy habit of prioritizing lesson planning keeps you in proactive, not reactive, mode.

Tip #1

Plan out your entire week at once a week before, and at the end of each day, set up for the next day.

Tip #2

Get in the habit of making copies and such for the entire week, if you can the week before.

This will help save you frustration and headache when the copier breaks down temporarily right when you need a set of copies (and it will).

Tip #3

If you are planning out a unit (two to eight weeks), simply break down the goals of each week and do daily plans and gather materials for each week one week before.

Tip #4

In Figure 3.2, you'll see how to optimally set up your time each week to keep a dynamic classroom while getting ahead with so many of the other tasks you have to do.

Figure 3.2

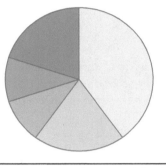

☐ Planning engaging curriculum for following week, grading, feedback to students (4 hours/week)

☐ Prepping curriculum (2 hours/week)

▨ Forming relationships with students (1 hour/week)

▨ Forming relationships with parents (1 hour/week)

▨ Miscellaneous teacher tasks (2 hours/week)

Source: Pariser and DeRoche, *Real Talk About Time Management* (2020).

You may feel the impulse to . . .	Take a deep breath, and try this instead.
Put planning on the back burner and focus on tasks like calling parents.	Remember that prioritizing planning above anything else is the key to having fewer behavioral disruptions.
Base your lesson plans on student behavior and "what they can handle."	Know that all students deserve engaging, fun, and dynamic lessons.

Ask Yourself:

How do I get myself a week ahead with daily lesson planning? Is there a prep period each week I can set aside (without distractions) for weekly planning?

Notes

How Do I Keep Students on Task With Group Work?

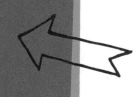

Group work can be your best friend or something you really dread. The fact is, most students love working in groups because humans are wired for connection. There's some planning that goes along with group work, and it's more than just asking students to push the desks together to get started. The first step is considering how you want to group the students. It's helpful to think: *Is the assignment I'm asking them to do more difficult than what most students in this classroom could do if asked to work independently?* If the answer is yes, heterogeneous groups are the way to go. This means students of different academic ability levels work in the same group to help one another. The advantage of grouping students heterogeneously is that each group most likely has both a student who might need a bit of support and a student or two who can help propel the group forward. Also, when giving opportunities for students to work collaboratively, groups of four to five students are usually the most beneficial and productive.

You will notice that some classes work better together than others. This could be because there are more interpersonal learners in a classroom or the students happen to be friends. If you have a class where group work is not going as smoothly as expected, consider assigning students group roles. Roles can be as follows:

- Group leader
- Encourager (humorously referred to as cheerleader)
- Includer (makes sure everybody is participating)
- Recorder
- Reporter (reports progress to the teacher)

Let groups decide who will do each role. This way, they will take more ownership of it. Urge students to switch roles each time they do group work and take on a new role every once in a while. For example, Aurelia shouldn't always be the leader, even though the students always naturally choose her. Every student in the class should get a chance to experience leadership and different roles. The roles serve as a scaffold for being able to work effectively together in a group, so when your class no longer needs the roles, feel free to remove them. Be clear that group members are to physically stay with their group, even when they are finished, and post a list of what they can do when they are finished so you can point to it if/when they ask. This will prevent the students from wandering around the room and possibly distracting other groups.

Tip #1

Consider arranging desks in groups before the students come into the room.

Tip #2

If students get to choose where their groups sit, ask students to make sure groups are at least five feet (one body length) away from one another to keep focus within each group.

Keep in Mind

Group work helps set the students up for success in the real world because almost all professions require that people be able to work with others to get a project or task finished.

INSTRUCTION

Tip #3

As groups are working, rotate around the room to answer questions and facilitate where needed.

Tip #4

Consider setting a timer for the amount of time they have to complete the group work and projecting the timer on a document camera so groups stay on task and engaged and pace themselves accordingly. A timer also creates a sense of urgency with the work.

Tip #5

Consider doing a mini lesson on conflict resolution, the importance of "carrying your weight" in a group, or active listening before starting group work.

You may feel the impulse to . . .	Take a deep breath, and try this instead.
Stop group work because many students do not stay on task.	Consider using a daily rubric and daily point system that can help support on-task behavior. Students can keep this form and have it out on their desks as they are working.
Get frustrated when students constantly need clarification on what they should do while in groups.	Provide both verbal and written instructions with group work. Perhaps project the directions large on your screen so every student can see.
Get frustrated when groups are too loud, and yell over the noise.	Instead of adding to the chaos, simply walk over to the loud group and politely ask them to lower their voices so others can focus. Remember, volume can also mean excitement and passion in group work!

Ask Yourself:

What social skills are students learning when working in groups? (You may even consider explicitly teaching these skills, like conflict resolution or active listening, quickly before students start working.)

Notes

_____

_____

_____

_____

_____

_____

_____

What If a Student Finishes Their Work Early?

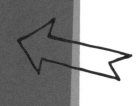

We focus so much on creating engaging lessons that incorporate collaborative work groups, yet we often forget to plan what to do with early finishers. Being proactive about what early finishers should do is a key ingredient to effective behavior management. If you are doing project-based learning, students will always have something to do, as they can add artistic flair to their project or work on the next step of their project or even offer a classmate peer feedback on a project.

However, sometimes students are just finished with their work. In this case, it's useful to offer choices on what students can do and have those choices written out so they can see. If you notice students are off task or sitting with nothing in front of them when they are done, you can simply point to the board where the choices are written. Being able to just point makes your life a lot easier because you don't have to keep repeating yourself and other students will not get distracted.

If two or more students are finished early, consider having them work together on an extension activity. This can mix up different groups of students and form connections between students who might not normally collaborate. Provide activities that represent cultures from around the world. For example, if you are doing a poetry unit, you could have poems from many different countries that students can study and explore together.

Here are some helpful ideas for early finishers:

Agency and Identity

Offering three to five choices of what students can do when they are finished allows them to explore and extend their interests, develop their critical thinking skills, and take ownership.

Early Finisher Options	Grade Level
Finish the artistic part of a project in project-based learning.	K–12
Organize binder and backpack and materials.	K–8
Classroom jobs—organize a part of the classroom.	K–8
Offer peer assessment, feedback, support—have students provide extra support to the groups that have not completed their project, or two students who are finished can trade assignments and give praise and critique/feedback.	4–12
In project-based learning, do ongoing projects.	K–12
Do extension activities—challenging activities related to content.	K–12
Play brain busters—educational games that emphasize critical thinking in your subject area.	K–12
Create music.	K–12
Writing center—create poems, journals, thank-you notes.	K–12
Independently read an enjoyable book—have books from all genres available in your classroom; this is especially important for math and science classrooms. It's a good idea to have your students always carry one with them.	K–12

Tip #1

Have a must/may chart so students know what they need to complete in that class period, and then they can have structured choices for what to do afterward. One column is the tasks the students *must* do in that class period, in order, and the other column is what they *may* choose to do when they are finished.

Tip #2

Consider having students use technology to go deeper and find out more information on the topic they just learned.

Tip #3

Keep reading materials around your room on topics that pertain to your classroom.

You may feel the impulse to . . .	Take a deep breath, and try this instead.
Not implement interactive learning activities for fear of what an administrator may think.	Indicate the connection between the content objective and activity objective. Have students identify or reiterate how the game connects to the content objective. For example, research has shown that play and team building are critical throughout a child's development.
Give students busywork to keep them engaged.	Busywork sounds like a great idea, but it works for only a moment. Students will be motivated to be actively engaged when you truly engage them in activities that capture their imagination and inspire them to use their critical and strategic thinking skills. Your students can also tell when a teacher is just assigning busywork.

Ask Yourself:

How does this extension activity connect to the content objective or help the student succeed academically?

Notes

What Are Some Teaching Strategies That Are More Engaging, Fun, and Collaborative Than Direct Instruction?

> Once I took the time to record myself teaching, it became apparent that I was doing all the talking and doing for my students. I began to engage my learners in more active learning methods and not as much direct instruction. This lessened the off-task behavior. I noticed I had more time to help students on an individual basis. And I was not as exhausted at the end of the day!
>
> —MRS. G., NINTH-GRADE MATH TEACHER

Think of direct instruction as a good old-fashioned lecture with or without visuals. Direct instruction can be effective, but it has a time, place, and limit. If you are teaching elementary school, a good rule of thumb is to limit direct instruction to 5- to 10-minute chunks. Middle schoolers can handle about 15 to 20 minutes, and high schoolers about 20 to 25 minutes. After that, students are often checking out and your energy—and much of the lesson—is wasted.

The good news is that we've come a long way from the "only lecture" days, and there are a plethora of highly engaging, fun, and collaborative teaching strategies that help students access the same amount of learning (often even more). Classrooms that embrace these types of teaching and learning activities have happier teachers and more engaged students. Doing this type of teaching also helps your class grow together as a community of learners and makes you more of a facilitator instead of an expert, as students start taking ownership of their learning—and most likely have some fun while doing so. When learning this way, students will feel more empowered to use their voices and, in turn, will learn your concepts on a deeper level. All students should always be able to participate and none should be excluded from fun and collaborative learning activities. These activities also teach students how to work together, solve conflict, and engage with different personality styles, which are important life skills.

The first or even second time using these teaching strategies, make sure you go over the instructions in written and also verbal form. Some students may need both until they get comfortable with these activities.

The table that follows provides some helpful ways students can learn concepts in an engaging and collaborative way:

Name of Activity	What It Looks Like in a Classroom	Purpose(s)
Socratic seminar	Students sit in a circle, read a text, and prepare with written notes. Then the teacher facilitates by asking open-ended questions to guide a student discussion.	• Students gain a deeper understanding of a text. • Empowers students to use their voices. • Teaches active listening skills.
Class brainstorms	Class thinks aloud together about a concept, and ideas are recorded for everybody to see. Brainstorm can be revisited at the end of the class to show how much students learned about a concept in one class period.	• Values student voices by writing all thoughts down on a collective brainstorm. • Gives teacher knowledge on what students already know about a concept before it is taught.
Carousel activity	Different questions are hung around the room on chart paper, and each student has a marker. Students add their input on the chart and rotate at a signal from the teacher, such as a bell, a fun song, or even the teacher saying "rotate" loudly.	• Gets students moving. • Can be an engaging way to share materials the whole class can use, such as answers to the question, "What are powerful transitions that can be used in an essay?" • Can be an engaging way to answer questions such as, "What do you think about . . . ?"
Station learning	Stations are set up around the room and usually numbered (either led by a teacher, co-teacher, student, technology, or self-instructed). It's helpful to mix it up. Student groups of four to five are practicing different concepts at once. Groups rotate to the next station when a timer goes off.	• Gets students moving. • Students can work collaboratively in each station. • Keeps student attention longer. • Keeps students task switching at a healthy pace, because when they move, they switch tasks. • Keeps student attention, as each station is a bit different.
Jigsaw	Student groups each take a part of a text to dissect, then come back together and teach their part to the entire class.	• Summarizes a longer text or document when it is not necessary for every student to read the entire text.
Inner-outer discussion	Similar to a Socratic seminar, but the outside circle is sitting with their backs turned to the inner circle and listening intently to take notes.	• Students gain a deeper understanding of a text. • Empowers students to use their voices. • Teaches active listening skills.

Name of Activity	What It Looks Like in a Classroom	Purpose(s)
Gallery walks	Hang up student work—drawings, poems, or any other creation—around the room, then students walk around silently to view one another's work. They can put praise or comments on sticky notes next to the work. This can be done walking around the desks. (Be sure to teach students about constructive comments to avoid negative or insulting notes, and ask students to write their names next to their positive comments to help create a community of learners.)	• Helps create a community of learners. • Students get to see everybody's work efficiently and with little effort from the teacher. • Students are all moving around the classroom.
Class debates	Class debates a concept you are teaching that might have two sides.	• Teaches active listening. • Students explore real-world issues. • Students practice compassionate listening. • Students' voices are heard. • Students can become more engaged in a concept they are learning.
Parallel instruction	Two adults are each teaching a concept the same way at the same time to half the class in heterogeneous groups. It usually works best if the teachers are facing away from each other on opposite sides of the room so the voices don't carry over each other.	• Students are taught in smaller groups, usually leading to more interaction between the instructor and the students.
Small-group instruction	Students are with an adult and usually being retaught a concept or provided extra support on a concept.	• This is a powerful method for students who have fallen behind, need extra support, or could benefit from a concept being taught in a different way.
Worksheet cut-up	Cut up your worksheet and place each section at a station. Have the students walk around to complete the worksheet to get movement in the lesson.	• Gets students moving and adds a layer of creativity and collaboration.

(Continued)

INSTRUCTION

(Continued)

Name of Activity	What It Looks Like in a Classroom	Purpose(s)
Reciprocal teaching	Students get the opportunity to be the teachers with a small group of students. The teacher sets students up for success by modeling how to guide group discussions with reading comprehension strategies.	• Empowers students by giving them opportunities to lead. • Students become aware of their own cognitive processes while reading a text. • Promotes student reading comprehension.

You may feel the impulse to . . .	Take a deep breath, and try this instead.
Not try any of these learning strategies for fear of losing control.	Keep in mind that we all learn from our mistakes and that's how we become our best teacher selves. Mistakes are okay and part of the learning process in a growth mindset.
Not try a strategy again if it flops.	Reflect on what went poorly, and make it better next time.
Mostly do direct instruction because that is what you are comfortable with.	Keep in mind that most of your students learn better with only a bit of direct instruction along with these strategies proactively planned into the lesson.
Not try these strategies because they are too much work.	Realize that when you start to use these strategies, your students actually do most of the work during class; you just do a bit more prep beforehand.

Ask Yourself:

How can I incorporate a new teaching/learning strategy better next time?

Notes

_____

Recap: Try This Tomorrow

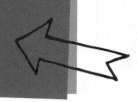

Each of these strategies takes little prep and can help you design engaging, fun, and collaborative learning for students.

- To keep students on task while doing group work, project a timer as well as the written directions on a document camera while students are working so they can monitor their own pacing and progress and keep a sense of urgency.
- Add an element of structured choice in your lesson to increase student ownership of and engagement in the learning.
- Consider assigning group roles with group work.
- When students are using technology, be sure to add a purposeful pause so students can also collaborate. This can mean they stop their technology projects and simply show each other what they are doing for a few minutes to assess each other and offer helpful feedback. Learning is still a social activity, even with technology.
- Get students up and moving at least a few times a week during the lesson. This can look like a gallery walk, station learning, a carousel activity, or even a class debate.
- Consider adding a competitive edge to lessons or projects to add some fun and an extra layer of engagement.
- Use a sticky note to write down tasks that pop into your head as you are lesson planning. Address them later.
- Post a must/may chart that lists a column of what they need to do and then a column of what they can choose to do if they finish early.
- Try a Socratic seminar or carousel activity.

Notes

INSTRUCTION

chapter FOUR

HOW CAN I MAKE ASSESSMENTS WORK FOR ME AND MY STUDENTS?

Imagine This

Your students are motivated to use the consistent, recurring academic feedback you give them to learn concepts on a deeper level. You are constantly assessing your students in creative ways when teaching a concept. You also use this data to inform your instruction and have the skill to do so. Because you do this, you catch more students before they have a chance to get lost in the material. Your students feel academically supported as well as challenged in your classroom.

You're not overwhelmed with grading, because you give real-time feedback in class and students have multiple opportunities to give feedback to one another when completing major assignments. Because of this, higher quality work is turned in.

Your students know they are in a community of learners, and they help one another succeed academically. This is because you have created an affirming classroom culture since day one.

You are comfortable assessing students' understanding both in person and online. You use class polls and other technology purposefully to assess as you are instructing.

You think creatively and critically about how to use assessments to inform instruction and have the skill to differentiate instruction when needed. This increases engagement for students as they are given tiered levels of support to reach the same understanding of a concept or complete a complex task. Students with Individualized Education Plans in your class receive the appropriate modifications and accommodations they are entitled to.

Assessments are no longer a four-letter word for both you and your students. They work. This can be your reality.

A thriving, dynamic classroom has a teacher who is constantly assessing their students' learning. Assessments used to be thought of only as the "end-of-a-unit" test or smaller quizzes. Education has progressed rapidly in the past decade, especially surrounding the concept of assessments: how they look, how often they are given, and how the data are used. Yes, sometimes "sit by yourself and answer multiple-choice or short-answer questions or write an essay" assessments, otherwise known as traditional assessments, are still given, but oftentimes assessments can look different. Let's take a look at how assessments can work for you as well as your students.

In this chapter about making assessments work for you and your students, the following questions will be answered:

- ☐ **What are engaging ways to check for understanding?**
- ☐ **What does effective feedback look like—and how does it fit with other assessments?**
- ☐ **When and why should I use rubrics?**
- ☐ **What do I do with assessment data?**
- ☐ **Why should I use assessments to differentiate instruction?**
- ☐ **What does differentiation look like in a classroom?**
- ☐ **What are some creative ways to assess in a virtual learning environment?**
- ☐ **How and why would I do peer conferencing?**

What Are Engaging Ways to Check for Understanding?

In short, a check for understanding is just that: You check to see if your students understand a concept you taught or directions for what they are about to do. A check for understanding is the simplest form of assessment. You are discovering what they get or what you might need to address again or in a different way. That's it!

Have a quick check for understanding written in your lesson plans for after a concept is taught. It's easy to forget but so important. You'll want to do this to see which students couldn't access the material. If only a few seem like they need more clarification, pull those students into a small group. If about half the class does not understand, empathetically reteach the lesson, perhaps in a slightly different way, or do an activity to help clarify the concept.

Be sure when you do a check for understanding, all students are participating. Not participating isn't an option. So while asking one student a question about what they understood at the end of a lesson can be beneficial, it's not entirely the best, because what about the rest of the students? You need to see where all students are in the learning process. Some students might need a little extra nudge to participate. Lack of participation can also be a red flag that they don't understand the content.

Some students may try to "hide" during a check for understanding if they are shyer, perhaps have a slight language barrier, or just aren't confident in what you taught. This is why checks for understanding with 100 percent participation are important. It's just as, or even more, important that you see who doesn't understand the material as who does.

Engaging Ways to Check for Understanding With 100 Percent Participation

Thumbs-Up/Thumbs-Down

Example: Ask students to tell you if they understand what they are supposed to do for the next 15 minutes by giving you a thumbs-up ("I understand"), thumbs-down ("I don't understand"), or thumb to the side ("I'm unsure"). When you start the activity, ask the students who didn't have their thumbs up to come to your desk so you can re-explain the directions. (Please note, this is a great quick assessment, but do not rely solely on the data this produces; students will often put their thumbs up so they are not "found out" for not understanding the material. This is good for checking on directions, but not necessarily for comprehension of content.)

Whiteboards

Example: Students each have a small whiteboard. You ask questions about what was just taught, and each student writes their answer on the whiteboard and holds it up.

Exit Tickets

Example: Students answer questions about the concept taught that day and hand it in to the teacher before they exit the classroom. Students who didn't fully understand can be pulled into a small group the next day to be retaught or to practice a concept.

You may feel the impulse to . . .	Take a deep breath, and try this instead.
Ask the class, "Are there any questions?" after a lesson.	Ask, "So what have I not made clear?" or "So what are you wondering?" Students (and adults) find it much more emotionally safe to admit to *wondering something* rather than *having a question* (Harris, 2021).
Move on quickly if students don't answer a question posed to the class, to avoid that awkward silence.	Offer plenty of wait time. Waiting as long as three to five seconds results in more students responding—and they respond at higher levels of thinking (Gage & Berliner, 1992).

Ask Yourself:

Am I checking for understanding at least once every lesson?

Notes

ASSESSMENT

This video, *Austin's Butterfly: Building Excellence in Student Work* (Berger, 2012), shows the transformational power of effective feedback to improve student work quality.

https://vimeo .com/38247060

Access and Equity

Using a rubric to assist grading and feedback can help prevent subconscious biases toward a student who understands the concept but might have a slight language barrier in communicating it in writing. This is because on a rubric, some of the sections grade the content knowledge and others grade the grammar and mechanics. For more on rubrics, see the next section in this chapter.

Before we focus on feedback, specifically, it's important to know the differences among assessment, grading, and feedback, and how each is used in the classroom. These are separate but complementary practices, although they're often conflated. The box that follows breaks each down for you.

Assessment

Purpose: To check to see if students understand what was taught; these can be informal, formative assessments that take place throughout a lesson or unit, and they can be more formal, summative measures, like an end-of-unit test or a year-end standardized test.

What it can look like in a classroom: *formative*—quick check for understanding, written responses to gauge understanding, exit tickets, whiteboard games; *summative*—end-of-unit tests, essays, and the like.

Grading

Purpose: Assigning points or a letter grade to represent how a student understood the material; helps teachers, schools, and parents know how close the student has come to meeting learning standards but should not be assumed to be a total picture of a student's ability.

What it can look like in a classroom: Giving a student a letter grade on an assignment, giving a student a letter grade on a test or quiz, giving a student a number of points earned on an assignment or test

Feedback

Purpose: Used as a basis for improvement and goal setting.

What it can look like in a classroom: Written comments on an assignment, a short conference with a student to orally give descriptive feedback, peer conferencing

Feedback is one of the most powerful tools for learning. According to an October 2018 report listing 250 influences on student achievement, pulled from 1,500 meta-analyses of 90,000 studies involving 300 million students, feedback was rated as a factor that would "considerably raise student achievement" (Hattie, 2018). The more constructive (and informed) feedback students receive, whether it comes from you *or their classmates*, the better.

However, thorough feedback takes time. One way to tackle this issue is to do some of your feedback in class, whether it is peer–peer or student–teacher assessment. Peer-to-peer feedback helps you create a community of learners who support one another in the process. Providing some feedback in real time also increases connections in your classroom and creates a community of learners who help and support one another, and gives you that bit of extra time on nights and weekends. Real-time feedback helps keep a growth mindset in your students because they are not only working toward an end grade. They are receiving feedback to support their growth as learners.

For longer writing assignments and essays, teach your students how to peer-conference one another's work a few times throughout the construction period before they submit the work to you. This can be a class activity you all do together, leading to higher quality work being turned in and less time spent grading. (There's a section on peer assessment later in this chapter.) Catlin Tucker, a former Teacher of the Year in Sonoma County, California, recommends meeting with individual students at a dedicated feedback station while they're working on their writing. She spends about three minutes per student, focusing on two or three specific skills at a time instead of every aspect of their paper (Tucker, 2017).

Here are some useful ideas for delivering constructive feedback:

- Start feedback with "I" statements. Example: "I notice here you solved the multiplication problem by . . ."
- If possible, give the students time to respond so it's a back-and-forth conversation.
- Ask students to jot down a few steps to work on. If it's not written down, students (and you) can easily forget.
- Make a feedback sandwich: Start with praise, then add constructive feedback, then end with praise and expression of the belief that the student can do it. The student will leave feeling empowered.

Weak Feedback Versus Strong Feedback

Weak Feedback	Strong Feedback
• Great job!	• In your paragraph two, you mentioned . . . What are your thoughts on . . . ?
• Excellent work!	• I admire the hard work you put into this assignment and the fact that you self-regulated to stay on pace. I also see that you used the feedback in peer conferencing to improve your grammar, and the improvement shows.
• Well done, excellent work.	• Your sentence structure was strong. Perhaps next time you can consider using a bit more academic writing to really make your essays shine.
	• Thank you for taking the time to organize your thoughts in this essay. It's clear that you understand the flow of an essay. It might be a useful idea to also use a thesaurus to increase the rigor of the vocabulary used in your writing. I'd be happy to help with that if needed!

ASSESSMENT

What Does Effective Feedback Look Like—and How Does It Fit With Other Assessments?

87

Great Resources

- Book: Hattie, J., & Clarke, S. (2019). *Visible learning: Feedback*. Routledge.
- Book: Johnson, M. (2020). *Flash feedback: Responding to student writing better and faster—without burning out*. Corwin.
- Book: Tepper, A., & Flynn, P. (2019). *Feedback to feed forward: 31 strategies to lead learning*. Corwin.
- Book: Tepper, A., & Flynn, P. (2020). *Learner-focused feedback: 19 strategies to observe for impact*. Corwin.
- Blog post: O'Connell, M. J., & Vandas, K. L. (2016, May 24). Feedback—it's everywhere, but is it good? *Corwin Connect*. https://corwin-connect.com/2016/05/feedback-everywhere-good/

You may feel the impulse to . . .	Take a deep breath, and try this instead.
Give letter grades without feedback.	Remember that feedback is one of the most powerful tools of learning. Be sure to give students time to read and dissect your written feedback during the process of learning, before they receive a grade. This way feedback is constructive and supportive, and is more likely to stick.
Get overwhelmed by your grading pile.	Decrease your grading pile by knowing you do *not* have to grade everything. Grade items that prove mastery of a concept you are teaching. Offer feedback and use quick assessments for all other items.
Get overwhelmed because you have so much to grade.	Try having students pair up and give feedback to each other before they complete an assignment. For more on peer review, see the final section in this chapter. Student–student feedback is a powerful opportunity for growth.

Ask Yourself:

How can you add more real-time feedback in your units to decrease grading time and improve quality of student work?

Notes

When and Why Should I Use Rubrics?

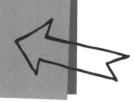

> Rubrics aren't just for summative evaluation. They can be used as a teaching tool as well. When used by students as part of a formative assessment, they can help students understand both the holistic nature and/or specific analytics of learning expected, the level of learning expected, and then make decisions about their current level of learning to inform revision and improvement (Reddy & Andrade, 2010).
>
> —BERKELEY CENTER FOR TEACHING & LEARNING (N.D.)

Long gone are the days when students simply completed a major assignment, handed it in, and then received a grade. Rubrics, yes, are used at the end to grade a major assignment or project, but they are also used during the creation process of the assignment.

This way the student knows exactly what is expected of them. Students can be given examples and non-examples of what is expected of them for each category in the rubric. Consider doing a class activity having students score an example of a high-scoring project or paper as well as an example of a low-scoring one so all students know what is expected of them. Students usually have fun during this type of project. When you take time to go over the rubric in class, students are more empowered to academically succeed on the assignment.

Students can also help co-create a rubric in class! This means you would leave some of the boxes blank and have students help you write them in as a lesson. Rubrics can also act as a scaffold for English language learners so they can see a breakdown of what is needed in an essay. It can act as a road map to success. Rubrics "level the playing field," because all students know what is expected of them in an assignment or project. Also, rubrics are a powerful tool to defend a grade to a disgruntled parent. The parent can see exactly where the student may have missed a few points and help the student get there next time. Rubrics can be used in peer conferences as well as self-evaluations as students are completing an assignment or project.

Keep in Mind

Simply put, the first time a student sees a rubric is not at the end of a project. In fact, ideally a student should see the rubric as the assignment or project is introduced.

Helpful examples of rubrics:

Figure 4.1 Example Rubric 1

SCORE	4	3	2	1
VOICE	Sounds confident, convincing, and compelling Reactions and feelings are well stated Uses formal writing that is mature	Sounds confident Reactions and feelings are clear Uses formal writing that is grade-level appropriate	Attempts to sound confident Reactions and feelings are somewhat well stated Writes informally	Unclear sense of audience and purpose
WORD CHOICE	Uses powerful, compelling words throughout the entire essay	Uses powerful, compelling words in most of the essay	Attempts to use powerful and compelling words in the essay	Limited vocabulary Words used incorrectly
STRUCTURE	Purposeful and powerful sentence structure Effective use of signal transition words and quotations that support the ideas in the essay	Strong sentence structure Clear use of signal transition words and quotations that support the ideas in the essay	Weak sentence structure Attempts to use signal transition words and quotations that support the ideas in the essay	Little or no sense of sentence structure
CONVENTIONS	Free of errors in quotation mark usage and citations Free of errors in comma usage Punctuates names of books and texts correctly Many errors in spelling and grammar	Minor errors in quotation mark usage and citations Minor errors in comma usage Punctuates names of books and texts correctly Minor errors in spelling and grammar	Many errors in quotation mark usage and citations Many errors in comma usage Attempts to punctuate names of books and texts correctly Many errors in spelling and grammar	Limited understanding of grade-appropriate spelling, grammar, and punctuation

Areas of strength:

Areas of growth:

Additional comments:

Source: Pariser and DeRoche, *Real Talk About Time Management* (2020).

Answers to Your Biggest Questions About Creating a Dynamic Classroom

Figure 4.2 Example Rubric 2

Persuasive Essay

My partner's persuasive essay . . . (check all that apply)

YES	NO	VOICE
		Sounds confident
		Uses formal language
		Reactions and feelings are well stated

Comments (suggestions, praise, room for improvement)

YES	NO	WORD CHOICE
		Uses powerful and compelling language

Comments (suggestions, praise, room for improvement)

YES	NO	STRUCTURE
		Has purposeful and powerful sentence structure
		Uses transition words effectively
		Uses quotations that clearly support the author

Comments (suggestions, praise, room for improvement)

YES	NO	CONVENTIONS
		Uses quotation marks correctly
		Uses commas correctly
		Uses punctuation in book titles correctly
		Uses correct spelling and grammar

Comments (suggestions, praise, room for improvement)

Source: Pariser and DeRoche, *Real Talk About Time Management* (2020).

You may feel the impulse to . . .	Take a deep breath, and try this instead.
Not create a rubric and just assign grades.	Remember that using a rubric can help you defend a grade to a student or parent and also will help students hand in higher quality work, because they have more direction.
Not have the rubric ready before introducing the project or assignment.	Know that giving students the rubric beforehand will produce higher quality work (saving you time and headache later) since they will have a road map of what is expected.
Not create a rubric because it's too laborious.	Know that a rubric will be your biggest support when defending a grade to a parent or student. It's hard to argue with a well-made rubric.
Not use a rubric and then get frustrated when many students fail an assignment.	Keep in mind that rubrics are a powerfully effective way for students to assess and peer-assess their work as they are creating. This leads to few or very few students failing a major assignment.

Ask Yourself:

How can I make sure students have a rubric as they are starting a major assignment or project, and use it as a teaching tool?

Notes

What Do I Do With Assessment Data?

> Assessment is the link between teaching and learning. Robust assessment systems allow teachers to make informed decisions about their impact and to adjust the learning experiences of students based on the evidence they collect. In essence, assessments provide teachers an opportunity to be an evaluator of their impact and can guide the future instruction that students experience.
>
> —DOUGLAS FISHER, NANCY FREY, VINCE BUSTAMANTE, AND JOHN HATTIE, *THE ASSESSMENT PLAYBOOK FOR DISTANCE AND BLENDED LEARNING* (2020, P. 1)

A good rule of thumb is to take some time in the beginning of the school year to look at the assessment data for your incoming students, if those data are available. Use the observations to help guide instructional planning and decisions, not to judge. Remember, assessment data isn't the stopping point, but it can be the beginning point. Some students have test anxiety, do not perform well on standardized assessments but still know the concepts, or perhaps were just tired that day. Use the data as a starting point but not a way to label a student indefinitely.

Assessment data could come from a major assessment, a state-mandated assessment, or simply performance on any assignment. It's really anywhere students were asked to show what they know. Use those data about what students know to inform your next steps in the classroom.

Tip #1

Assessments can also be used to empower students. If students did not score well on an assessment, have them create an action plan for improvement. Be sure to give them opportunities to check back in on their progress from time to time.

Tip #2

Assessment data can be used to reteach a concept in a different way to a small group that scored low on a test.

Tip #3

Use state-mandated assessment data from the previous school year to create heterogeneous seating charts in the beginning of a school year.

ASSESSMENT

Tip #4

Assessment data can be used to guide station learning. Areas where students overall scored low or did not perform well can be a station. For more on station learning, see Chapter 3.

Tip #5

Assessment data can be used to know what concepts need to be retaught. Invite your co-teacher (if applicable) to reteach a concept to a small group. Students might benefit from hearing somebody else explain a concept.

Tip #6

Assessment data can be used to invite a student to reteach a concept to the class or a small group. Students might benefit from hearing another student explain it. Also, if a student can teach it, they know it. Use this tactic sparingly.

You may feel the impulse to . . .	Take a deep breath, and try this instead.
Move on even if many students did not do well on an assessment because you have so much to cover in a year.	Take a day or two and use assessment data to place students in small groups, and reteach the concept in a different way.
Get frustrated if most of the class did not understand a concept.	If most of the class did not understand a concept, please remember that this is where the teacher has an ethical responsibility to revisit it or reteach it differently.
Give back a test or quiz at the end of class, not allowing students a chance to reflect on their feedback.	With major assignments, give students guidance and time in class to self-reflect on what they did well and what they are still unsure of, and to dissect the teacher's feedback. This is a powerful learning opportunity. Self-reflection can look like notes jotted on a graphic organizer, discussion with a peer, or some other form of reflection. This also ensures that students are taking the time to dissect the feedback that probably took you a lot of time to give.

Ask Yourself:

How am I using assessment data to make decisions about my teaching?

Notes

Why Should I Use Assessments to Differentiate Instruction?

> Today's effective teachers must not only differentiate instruction to facilitate their students' acquisition of the core curriculum content, but they must do so much more.
>
> —JACQUELINE S. THOUSAND, RICHARD A. VILLA, AND ANN I. NEVIN, *DIFFERENTIATING INSTRUCTION* (2015, P. XVII)

We differentiate instruction because, unless you have a class of all Advanced Placement learners, you most likely teach students with a very wide range of academic abilities who require different paces of learning. Students need different levels of support to reach the same goal of mastery of a concept or completion of a project or major assignment. Differentiation also allows for smaller groups, so the teacher can help students with a more personalized method rather than only full-class instruction.

Teachers can use quick assessments to inform their decisions regarding the best possible path for each student to gain the same mastery of a concept, or a different level of support to gain the same completion of a major assignment. Differentiation simply means you are teaching differently to different small groups. This could be teaching a different topic in each group or changing up the level of support to meet your students where they are academically.

This video (Edutopia, 2021) shows how differentiation can help the teacher meet the wide variety of student levels.

https://www.youtube.com/watch?v=GkZUXdTOWcY

Access and Equity

Differentiation allows more students to access the curriculum because each student is receiving the level of support they need when practicing a concept or completing an assignment.

Keep in Mind

Differentiation is all about adding in different amounts of support for each small group in the learning process, rather than lowering expectations for different sets of students.

A key element of doing differentiation successfully is beginning with assessment, a diagnostic tool, and gathering data, which gives the teacher background knowledge of where to begin to plan for differentiation. This can be information from a student's Individualized Education Plan (IEP), reading level, test data, or even student interest form. Most of the time, you'll organize the groups ahead of the lesson where differentiation occurs, because the groups are based on some sort of assessment. For example, this can be as simple as jotting down the number of paragraphs students have completed on their essay, then forming groups based on that the next day. Students who have written zero to two paragraphs are in one group with the most adult support, students who have written three to four are in another group with lighter support, and students who are well on their way are in an independently working group sitting together, where they can help one another with ideas if needed.

An additional way to differentiate, beyond assessment data, is allowing students to advocate for themselves. This would mean letting students choose their groups based on the level of support they think they need. This is a powerful way to empower students. Using the same essay example from above, you could say, "If you feel confident to work on your own, sit in this group; if you are stuck on your first or second paragraph, sit in this group (the teacher will work with that group for higher level support); and if you want to collaborate with a peer, sit in this group." This works once in a while with certain assignments, and you can differentiate based on what group they choose.

Differentiation can also be powerful for students learning English as a new language, who can be given extra support in a group when writing an essay or doing another heavy language task. It's important that a group isn't just EL learners but any student who could use that level of support. Also, emerging bilingual students who are at a higher level of English language acquisition might not need this support and can be placed in a group that is not as heavily scaffolded.

Great Resource

Book: Thousand, J. S., Villa, R. A., & Nevin, A. I. (2015). *Differentiating instruction: Planning for universal design and teaching for college and career readiness* (2nd ed.). Corwin.

You may feel the impulse to . . .	Take a deep breath, and try this instead.
Not differentiate because all students should have the same expectations for the content.	Accept that students will need different levels of support to reach the same expectations. Learners today are more diverse than ever. Differentiation is a very effective way to give students different levels of support.
Get frustrated if students aren't engaging in a concept.	Keep in mind that differentiation offers more engagement, provides more opportunities to creatively think and collaborate with peers, and develops students' 21st-century skills, which is a critical component in student success.

Ask Yourself:

Have I used assessments or check-ins to plan for differentiation?

Notes

What Does Differentiation Look Like in a Classroom?

In differentiated instruction, students will have more access to an adult because they are in smaller groups. Contrarily, some students may have more autonomy, as they might be working in a group that does not have an adult leading it. Every student gets access to the support or independence they need. Typically students are in about three to four groups sitting together, getting different levels of support. There are a couple of different approaches as to when to implement differentiation in your instruction. You can teach the same material to the whole class and then differentiate for the practice part of the lesson, or the entire lesson can be at varying levels of challenge taught in a small-group setting that is based on student ability levels.

Model what students need to do to complete a task, then differentiate the levels of support students are given. For example, a teacher may model how to complete a science lab so students are able to perform the experiment. One group might work completely without support. Another group might have a teacher guiding them. And a third group may have a co-teacher or support adult heavily guiding them with a modified experiment per their IEP modifications. This is differentiation. Also, groups may be different sizes based on what students need. One group may be four students, one may be 15 students, and one may be 12 students.

How else can differentiated instruction look?

- Give students different levels of support on the same texts to access the material based on reading and comprehension levels.
- Offer students different levels of support to write an essay, based on their progress in completing a draft.
- Provide students different levels of support learning a math concept, based on a math assessment, offering a range of problems and levels of difficulty.
- Let students choose which group they go to based on student interest. Give the same level of support to each group with different topics. Remember that this type of differentiation does not group students homogeneously.

Tip #1

Differentiation students are usually in homogeneous small groups, each doing different learning activities on the same content, with tiered levels of support.

Tip #2

Grouping students based on interests is a fantastic way to differentiate and motivate students at the same time.

Tip #3

If students are grouped by interest, the same level of support might be given but on different texts or topics students choose.

Keep in Mind

When differentiating instruction, some sort of formative assessment informs the groups, and the groups will change every time.

Keep in Mind

If you have a co-teacher, a student teacher, or a paraprofessional or tutor, they can lead a group at the same time you lead a group, and one group that needs the least amount of support can work independently.

ASSESSMENT

Great Resources

- Book: Thousand, J. S., Villa, R. A., & Nevin, A. I. (2015). *Differentiating instruction: Planning for universal design and teaching for college and career readiness* (2nd ed.). Corwin.

- Book: Tomlinson, C. (2020). *How to differentiate instruction in academically diverse classrooms* (3rd ed.). ASCD.

You may feel the impulse to . . .	Take a deep breath, and try this instead.
Differentiate without homogeneous grouping.	Homogeneous grouping is the most efficient for differentiation of instruction. Not only can adults work with a group of students at once, but students can get help from one another within the groups, as they are all doing the same task. It also creates less isolation in the learning process.
Differentiate almost daily.	Differentiation is most beneficial if it's done only up to a few times a week. It's most beneficial if done with more difficult tasks, assignments, or concepts. Doing this too often can break up a whole class community, and certain students will begin to self-identify with a group.
Always have the second adult in your classroom working with the same students when you differentiate because they are comfortable with that.	Know that true differentiation requires purposeful and always-changing groups. Groups should be determined before the lesson, based on student needs. This way, students don't get identified or labeled and attached to a certain group. Also, sometimes the lead teacher works with the groups that need the most support, and sometimes it switches.

Ask Yourself:

How can I think differently about my content and add in a layer of differentiation, or perhaps a type of differentiation I've never tried before?

Notes

What Are Some Creative Ways to Assess in a Virtual Learning Environment?

When we think about virtual learning, we often think about a teacher talking to a video camera and students listening and soaking in information. Occasionally, a student can type a question into a chat box, and hopefully the teacher can address it. Since the beginning of the global pandemic in the 2020–2021 school year, virtual learning has come a long way. We have discovered more about how we can assess learning during a virtual lesson as well as after it. More awareness of technological advances allows for more ways to engage with virtual learners and to assess students during the learning process. Virtual learning doesn't change the amount we need to assess; we just have to think a little more creatively about how to do it. For example, you might offer students structured choices on how they complete an assignment in virtual learning. Students could choose among writing a traditional paper, creating a presentation on Google Slides, or perhaps even making a video that relays the same information and same amount of rigor.

Another important aspect of assessment is checking in with students frequently, because virtual learning is different from traditional in-person learning. Consider sending out a short student feedback Google Form every so often. Virtual learning is a fairly new concept, so students' feedback can help you assess how they are viewing and feeling about the class and the content. Also, virtual instructors often lose a sense of colleague collaboration and support, so student feedback keeps an open dialogue about the course from your only evaluators—your students.

Tip #1

Post a poll in the chat box regarding the content, to assess learning or simply to get student interaction.

Tip #2

Use Google Forms to assess efficiently. Post the link to the form in the chat box.

Tip #3

Thumbs-up/thumbs-down/thumbs to side (mentioned in a different use earlier in this chapter) can also be used if you see a video of the student. Ask the students to tell you how well they feel they grasped the material by showing you a thumb signal. You can consider pulling students into a private virtual breakout room (with you or a virtual co-teacher) to reteach or revisit the material.

Tip #4

Have students record a two- to three-minute video reflection answering guiding questions about the content.

ASSESSMENT

Tip #5

Students can create a PowerPoint presentation about a concept and deliver the presentation to the class virtually, just as they would in a brick-and-mortar classroom.

Tip #6

Use Padlet or Google Jamboard to have students answer a question or post their ideas on a concept in a shared class document.

This also helps build a community of learners in a virtual setting.

Tip #7

Virtual exit tickets can also be created with Google Forms.

Great Resources

Blog post: Fleming, N. (2020, October 1). 7 ways to do formative assessments in your classroom. *Edutopia.* https://www.edutopia.org/article/7-ways-do-formative-assessments-your-virtual-classroom

Book: Fisher, D., Frey, N., Bustamente, V., & Hattie, J. (2020). *The assessment playbook for distance learning.* Corwin.

You may feel the impulse to . . .	Take a deep breath, and try this instead.
Resort heavily to lecture style when teaching virtually because it's what you are most comfortable with.	Know that virtual assessment takes a bit of creative thinking but is highly informative to teachers.
Wait until the end of a virtual lesson to assess.	Remember that with technology you can assess quickly throughout the lesson with polls, Google Forms, or simply a thumbs-up or thumbs-down into a camera.

Ask Yourself:

How do I know that my students are learning the concepts I am teaching in a virtual environment?

Notes

How and Why Would I Do Peer Conferencing?

Do peer conferencing a few times, and you and your class will be hooked. It can work for any discipline and any grade level. This practice creates independent learners who will be ready to turn in their best efforts with the help of their peers. Using a system like this will not only save you time on grading but will also help the students produce higher quality work without your assistance.

All students should have the opportunity to assess one another's work. Peer conferencing empowers students, builds confidence, and encourages independence. Also, it helps create academic trust among students, which in turn creates a community of learners and takes some of the pressure off you. Students will get feedback from one another to strengthen their assignments and projects during the creation process. Peer conferencing can be done a few times throughout the creation of a longer writing piece or any other major project. One additional benefit of peer conferencing is that you will receive higher quality work at the end, and students will find joy in collaborating with one another.

How to set up peer conferencing:

Note: Peer conferencing takes about 30 minutes or more of class time.

1. Students pair up with whomever they like and trade work with each other. Urge them to pair up with somebody who will give them useful feedback.
2. Teacher gives students a checklist of what to look for in the work. If students are further along in the creation, a rubric can also be used. (Rubrics are discussed earlier in this chapter.)
3. Quietly reading work and giving written feedback: Students give written positive as well as constructive feedback (not directly on the student work). This can be done on a sticky note or graphic organizer.
4. *Important step* Discussion: Students take turns talking to each other about the feedback and can ask clarifying questions of each other.
5. Using feedback to improve work: Students use the oral and written feedback to improve quality of work. This should be done in class *immediately* after the peer conference.

When can I do peer conferencing?

- Writing an essay
- Completing a multistep project
- Building something in class
- Creating a piece of art in class

Agency and Identity

By evaluating the work of others and offering feedback, students will become better able to evaluate and improve their own work. Remember from Bloom's taxonomy that evaluation is one of the highest levels of critical thinking.

ASSESSMENT

You may feel the impulse to . . .	Take a deep breath, and try this instead.
Get frustrated if students aren't giving constructive feedback to each other.	Consider teaching a mini lesson on the benefits of respectful, constructive feedback with examples and non-examples. Use the video *Austin's Butterfly*, which can be found with QR Code 4.1. Showing this video is an enjoyable and fun way to launch peer conferencing.
Tell students to focus only on what needs to be improved in their partner's work.	Let students know that the positive comments are just as helpful as the constructive ones. They should leave the peer meeting empowered, not defeated.
Decide to quit peer feedback after the first time implementing, if things don't go well.	Try reviewing with students the expectations (keep them clear and concise), and have them practice one piece at a time.

Ask Yourself:

How can incorporating peer conferencing in my assignments help create a community of learners in my classroom and improve the quality of work turned in?

Notes

Recap: Try This Tomorrow

Each of these strategies takes little prep and can help guide you to making assessments work for you and your students.

- If students are working on an essay, dedicate one station each day to providing real-time feedback as they write.
- Before turning students loose on a task, ask them to tell you if they understand what they are supposed to do by giving you a thumbs-up, thumbs-down, or thumb to the side (they're a little unsure). When you start the activity, ask the students who didn't have their thumbs up to come to your desk so you can re-explain the directions.
- Use a quick interest form to group students by interest and differentiate instruction while completing a task on a concept.
- Utilize a co-teacher or another adult in the classroom to help lead a small group and differentiate instruction.
- Use assessment data to have students create academic goals for themselves.
- When teaching with technology, use class polls to take the pulse of the class and assess on the spot.
- If you're trying peer conferencing, quickly go over effective feedback and ineffective feedback with the class.
- Give students access to the rubric before they start the assignment or project to increase understanding of expectations and increase motivation. This will lead to higher quality work, which takes less time to grade.
- Use the rubric as a teaching tool and give students examples and non-examples of each category in the rubric so they can fully understand what they are being asked to do and the level of rigor.

Notes

ASSESSMENT

WHAT ARE THE THINGS I NEED TO KNOW . . . BUT ARE RARELY DISCUSSED IN A TEACHER TRAINING PROGRAM?

Imagine This

You absolutely love your job and can't imagine doing anything else for a living. You like going to work every day and are a dedicated professional who is valued by both your students and your colleagues. Yet your personal life is still thriving. You have not sacrificed your personal time out of school and know that this helps you show up for class each day more present and well balanced. You have so much to offer to your students and the lessons.

Yes, there are a few times throughout the year you do feel you lose your balance. In these cases, you are able to re-center yourself and understand the difference between stressors you can control and stressors out of your control. You know how to gracefully take action to minimize stressors you can control to regain your sense of balance. You have the skills to do this.

You know with conflict that may come up at school with another adult, you have choices in how you react and solve the conflict. This often makes your relationship with that colleague stronger in the long run as differences and misunderstandings are calmly and empathetically worked out.

You have a relationship of mutual respect with your administration. They support and admire the work you do in your classroom and often stop by to witness your students showcasing their projects and other academic presentations.

The parents and caregivers admire and support the work you have done with students since day one. You even know how to connect with parents if there is a language barrier. You have strategies for this.

However, once in a while there is a parent meeting that is more difficult than others. You approach these meetings prepared and have the skills to diffuse an angry or upset parent. You don't dread these meetings because you know most of the time it is a miscommunication, and at the end of these well-navigated meetings, you, the parent, and the student are all working on the same team again.

Yes, sometimes you have tasks you just can't seem to get started on or dislike a bit more than others. When this happens, you have strategies to help you get started and gain some momentum. You keep these strategies in your back pocket.

Yes, sometimes your lessons flop or something messes up during the school day. You know these mistakes or flops are what make you stronger and highlight opportunities for growth. You pick yourself back up with skill and ease. Your true strength as a teacher shines through in these moments.

You purposefully surround yourself with other teachers who are optimistic and have a positive energy, and you all make yourselves stronger as teachers with one another's help. You enjoy and admire your colleagues.

Your self-care is even scheduled into your calendar because you know it is a priority. This keeps you feeling good. This can all be your reality.

There are aspects of teaching about which others will tell you, "Oh, that just comes with time." Why does it have to take time to uncover these answers? The students you teach today deserve a teacher who knows the answers now and is better prepared earlier in their career. This chapter can help support and guide you through this maze and take the mystery out of it. These are issues that probably aren't in any teacher training or credentialing programs but are crucial to success, satisfaction, and longevity in this noble profession.

In this chapter, the following questions will be answered:

- ☐ **How do I keep a work/life balance?**
- ☐ **How do I make time for some serious self-care?**
- ☐ **What can I proactively do to avoid feeling overwhelmed or burned out?**
- ☐ **What if I have a conflict with a colleague?**
- ☐ **How can I build a supportive relationship with administrators?**
- ☐ **How do I work with a co-teacher effectively?**
- ☐ **How can I creatively get parent and caregiver support from day one?**
- ☐ **How do I build healthy parent and caregiver relationships?**
- ☐ **How do I navigate a difficult meeting with a parent or caregiver?**
- ☐ **How do I pick myself back up after I mess up?**
- ☐ **What small tweaks make a profound difference in my job satisfaction and overall well-being?**
- ☐ **What are some effective time-saving hacks?**

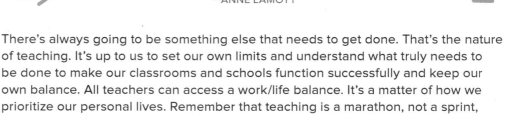

> *Almost everything else will work again if you unplug it for a few minutes, including you.*
>
> —ANNE LAMOTT

There's always going to be something else that needs to get done. That's the nature of teaching. It's up to us to set our own limits and understand what truly needs to be done to make our classrooms and schools function successfully and keep our own balance. All teachers can access a work/life balance. It's a matter of how we prioritize our personal lives. Remember that teaching is a marathon, not a sprint, and it's impossible to sprint an entire 26.2 miles. Yes, you would be faster in the beginning, but you wouldn't finish. (We will also discuss later in this chapter how to avoid burnout.)

Keeping a work/life balance not only helps you be your best teacher self; it also keeps you happier as a human being and oftentimes helps you thrive in the profession longer.

Keeping a work/life balance helps reduce stress and prevent burnout in the workplace. Chronic stress is one of the most common health issues in the workplace. It can lead to physical consequences such as hypertension, digestive troubles, chronic aches and pains, and heart problems.

Work/life balance is a bit different from self-care, which is discussed in the next section. Work/life balance means maintaining your social relationships and activities outside of work. And it means being proactive to enjoy a personal life, as difficult as that may seem the first few years. Maintaining a work/life balance requires you to pay attention to signals that the balance is off, too.

What could a healthy work/life balance look like?

- Keep friend and family relationships and obligations during the school year.
- When spending time with friends and loved ones, talk about something other than work.
- Make a point to schedule weekend outings, dinners, and time with others in advance.
- Spend time with your family or loved ones some nights instead of grading or lesson planning.
- Look for events, concerts, shows, or activities in your area and schedule them ahead of time with others. Make sure you keep these obligations and go have fun! These activities could even be with people from your work so you can get to know each other on a personal level.
- A few days a week, set a timer so you can try to be more consistent in the time you leave school, keeping promises to your family or loved ones.
- Consider not checking work emails on the weekends or after a certain time at night. It stops when you stop it.

Keep in Mind

Nobody enters the teaching profession planning to give up their work/life balance. But it can happen if you don't actively work to keep it.

Helpful reminders for why to keep a work/life balance:

- We show up more present for our students every day.

- We do not feel resentment toward our class for sacrificing our personal time.

- We have more emotional capital, patience, and energy to give.

- We are happier at work, leading to a happier classroom environment.

- We are more excited about our lessons, and in turn, our students are more engaged.

- We give our brains a break from the teaching thoughts that go through our heads. Our minds need to rest and think about something else for a bit.

You may feel the impulse to . . .	Take a deep breath, and try this instead.
Cancel plans with friends and family to get more done for your classroom.	Know that human beings need to maintain relationships with loved ones to function optimally and keep a work/life balance.
Work tirelessly trying to get everything done.	Keep in mind that you most likely will never get everything done. Do not feel guilty about stopping for the day when you need to stop.
Mindlessly start doing tasks without prioritizing them.	Be mindful to prioritize what needs to get done most urgently, and do that first. Creating lesson plans and prepping for instruction should always be a top priority. After this is complete, grading and other tasks should follow.
Make your personal life secondary.	Consider joining an organized sport or team (bowling, softball, etc.), or some other weekly activity that is prescheduled and forces you to unplug.

Ask Yourself:

- What part of my outside-of-work life do I want to focus on to stay balanced?
- What relationships or social activities in my life do I want to prioritize?

Notes

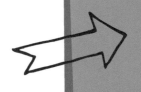

How Do I Make Time for Some Serious Self-Care?

> Practice self-care and nurture your needs as a person. It's important to identify passions outside of teaching and continue to pursue those as well. I now get monthly massages and pedicures; I practice meditation and being present in the moment; and I do things I love that make me feel most alive, such as writing poetry and going to the beach, concerts, and farmers' markets. When you honor your own needs, it allows you to feel more whole, therefore making you a better teacher for your students.
>
> —MRS. ZIMMERMAKER, EDUCATION SPECIALIST

What's the difference between work/life balance and self-care? Work/life balance is a state you achieve to balance your personal life with your work life, and self-care is taking the time to do the things that "fill your cup" when needed. Filling your cup is replenishing your mental, physical, and spiritual well-being. In our profession, self-care is particularly important. It's been noted that a teacher makes 1,500 decisions a day—more than brain surgeons (TeachThought, n.d.).

Self-care can look many different ways. It can be something as simple as taking a walk after school every day, getting out into nature on the weekends, spending time with friends and family, or simply keeping a gratitude journal at your desk. The more self-care, the better, and it doesn't have to break the bank.

The first thing you want to do when starting to think about self-care is make a list of five to ten things you like to do for yourself that fill your cup. Then keep this list handy. Plan one of these activities weekly to start. Schedule it as you would any other meeting, and try your best not to cancel it or schedule anything else in that time slot.

You could consider having a self-care buddy from your school. This would be somebody you get manicures/pedicures with, you go to an exercise class with, you take walks with, or is merely your accountability partner and checks in on you occasionally to see if you are taking enough time for self-care. Consider having the teachers and staff at your school start a social sports league such as softball, kickball, or even dodgeball to get a sweat in and unwind once a week, replenishing your physical selves and having some fun while deepening bonds and connections with staff.

Self-care can also look like using your personal days when needed, without guilt. You'll know when you need it. Many teachers do not use these days early in their teaching career, while experienced teachers often know taking these days to recharge is beneficial in the long run and to their overall well-being.

Keep in Mind

Seventy percent of employees say friendships at work are the most crucial element to a happy working life (Schawbel, 2018). Practicing self-care with a colleague or group is an opportune time to build these relationships and get to know your colleagues as human beings, not just educators.

In addition to taking time to fill your cup when needed, you can do proactive self-care. This looks like choosing healthy food options and making it a priority to practice bringing healthy lunches to school often. Eating healthy will make a noticeable difference in your energy levels, stamina, and overall patience and mental clarity throughout the school day.

Great Resource

Blog post: Gonzalez, J. (2017, June 19). Why it's so hard for teachers to take care of themselves (and 4 ways to start). *Cult of Pedagogy.* https://www. cultofpedagogy.com/ teacher-self-care/

Tip #1

Book social outings, concerts or activities, weekend trips, massages, or hair/nail appointments some time in advance so they cannot get pushed aside.

Tip #2

Bring a set of walking shoes or workout clothes to school with you or keep them in your classroom so you have to **change before you drive home**.

This ensures you will get that walk in or go to the gym before the couch calls to you.

You may feel the impulse to . . .	Take a deep breath, and try this instead.
Put self-care aside to get your grading pile complete.	Remember that the way we take care of ourselves will bleed into our teaching.
Skip lunches or eat unhealthy lunches at school for lack of time.	Take some time on the weekend to get healthy lunches at the store or prepare meals ahead of time so you can eat healthy with minimal effort during the week. Or start small and substitute one healthy food option a week.

Ask Yourself:

- What do I like to do outside of work that energizes me and helps me show up as a more present teacher? How can I schedule this into my calendar as I would any work obligation or meeting?
- What positive lifestyle change can I substitute for a harmful habit?

Notes

AGENCY

What Can I Proactively Do to Avoid Feeling Overwhelmed or Burned Out?

> *Overwork is not the cause of burnout. Burnout occurs when our heart is in one place and our work is in another. The passion dies and we no longer look forward to the work that previously gave us joy. Work is no longer rewarding. We are emotionally, psychologically, or physically exhausted.*
>
> —BARBARA BROCK AND MARILYN GRADY, *AVOIDING BURNOUT: A PRINCIPAL'S GUIDE TO KEEPING THE FIRE ALIVE* (2002, P. 6)

Let go of perfectionism. It's exhausting. It's important to know that there is a difference between just needing a break and starting to burn out. When you start to feel overwhelmed, commit to finishing a task that needs to be done, and celebrate after. Celebrate your successes or just take a break. There's nothing like rewarding yourself with a weekend getaway after a great semester.

But burnout is different. Preventing burnout is more than merely taking a weekend getaway. It's about being aware of the stages of burnout and creating systems in your life where you are getting enough nourishment for your emotional and physical health, knowing what you have to do and what you can set aside, committing yourself to your most meaningful work, and having a strong support system of friends and loved ones around you.

"According to a 2020 Gallup report [Wigert, 2020], 76% of respondents said they experience burnout at least sometimes. The good news? You can recover from burnout" (Goldberg, 2021). There are five stages of burnout (Simona, 2021; *What Are the 5 Stages of Burnout?* 2020):

Stage #1: The Honeymoon Phase

You have high job satisfaction and feel energized by the new tasks, and have a high level of commitment, energy, and productivity. You may take on more than you should.

Stage #2: Onset of Stress

Stress starts and optimism begins to fade a bit. Some days might seem tougher than others.

Stage #3: Chronic Stress

More intense symptoms of stress set in. The job may start to feel out of control. You may get sick more frequently and get angry over small issues. You may also start to distance yourself from social events and become apathetic, miss deadlines, and feel tired often.

Stage #4: Burnout

This phase is characterized by feeling a lack of fulfillment, neglecting your personal needs, increasing mental distance from your job, and having a pessimistic view of your work.

Stage #5: Habitual Burnout

This happens when you don't take time to recover from burnout. You are so used to this state, you may stop doing things you once enjoyed and experience chronic mental fatigue, chronic depression, and chronic sadness. It may affect your personal relationships as well.

Awareness is the key to prevention. If you need a break, then take a break. However, when you start to feel yourself burning out as described in the stages just described, that's the time to put systems in place to nourish your body and mind. If you ignore this feeling and keep working through it, you will become more and more disconnected from your passion, your work will not be high quality, and you will just be going through the motions. And that's when burnout sets in or becomes chronic. Creating these systems actually rejuvenates us, gets us back to our center, and helps us revisit the work with our true intention. Burnout isn't something that happens instantaneously; it's a gradual process that sets in slowly when we are ignoring the signs over a prolonged period of time.

Also, it's important that we can differentiate between healthy stress and unhealthy stress. A bit of healthy stress can help motivate you or create a sense of urgency to finish a project, or even inspire you and enhance your performance. Healthy stress is short-term.

Unhealthy stress is long-term and can have harmful effects on your body, such as hindering your ability to make decisions; taking away your desire to socialize with others; and causing poor concentration, mood swings, insomnia, anxiety, jitteriness, irritability, confusion, loss of energy, depression, headaches, high blood pressure, or even weight gain (to name a few).

Example of healthy stress: Your school is getting ready for an upcoming parents night, students are working to finish projects, and you have much to do to be ready to welcome the parents. You are temporarily working longer hours, but the students, you, and colleagues are all excited for the event, even though it's a lot of preparation.

Example of unhealthy stress: You feel undervalued by your administration. You constantly work longer hours because you have taken on more responsibilities than you can handle in a regular workday, and you have poor classroom management because you have little energy to give to your classes. You are constantly scrambling to make lesson plans at the last minute because you have too many other responsibilities at school. This has been going on for three years.

How to keep your fire alive:

- Keep yourself nourished physically and emotionally. Spend quality time with friends and loved ones.

- Learn how to speak up when your physical, mental, emotional, or spiritual reserves can't be spread any thinner.

- Know where you can spend less time on something and how to prioritize.

- Schedule self-care into your calendar.

- Ask for help when you need it.

- Get outside for 20 minutes a day, five days a week.

- Take a 10-minute walk around school as often as you can.

- Get in nature as often as possible.

- Actively work to build a strong community and support network around you.

- Get into a routine for exercise and healthy eating.

- Research different time management techniques.

- Actively work on creating a positive classroom culture (see Chapter 1).

- Take a personal day for mental health when you need it.

- Focus on successes. This will rewire your brain away from negativity.

- Keep your classroom neat and orderly to create a sense of calm.

- Delegate tasks that you can. You cannot and do not have to do everything.

Great Resources

- Blog post: Betz, A. (n.d.). Teacher burnout: Warning signs, causes, and tips on how to avoid. *Education Corner.* https://www.educationcorner.com/teacher-burnout.html

- Website: *Dave Stuart, Jr.* http://www.davestuartjr.com

You may feel the impulse to . . .	Take a deep breath, and try this instead.
Get annoyed or stressed about the same thing daily, over and over again.	Know your triggers, and avoid them if possible. What can you do differently to avoid them?
Say yes to everything you are asked to do, even if you know you do not have the capacity to do it.	Be comfortable politely declining a task you cannot take on.
Deal with stress by overeating, oversleeping, or just carrying the load.	Consider doing something that gets your body moving. A body in motion is out of emotion.

Ask Yourself:

Is this stress I'm feeling healthy or unhealthy stress? What's in my control that I can change?

Notes

What If I Have a Conflict With a Colleague?

> Simply said, anybody that works in an organization with other people has to learn how to have hard conversations. But we're not born with this skill. Oh yes, we can have great conversations, dancing around the point, hoping that the listener will infer our message and make changes. It happens to all of us, and often.
>
> —DOUG FISHER AND NANCY FREY (IN ABRAMS, *HARD CONVERSATIONS UNPACKED*, 2016, P. VII)

Schools are organizations that are filled with people all working toward a common goal. However, you will most likely have a conflict, perhaps only a minor one, with another colleague at some point in your career. One of the most important things to remember is that people who work in a school are generally compassionate. That is one of the factors that sets the profession apart from others. Teachers are not usually in it for the money or personal gain. They are in it for the kids. However, as the school year goes on, it can get stressful at times, teachers can get tired, and frankly sometimes teachers do not see eye to eye with one another. This is where the work has to come in.

Most important, handling conflict in a healthy way takes empathy. This means trying to see where the other person is coming from. Put yourself in their shoes for a few moments. Is there a perspective you might not be considering?

Now consider the stakes. If the outcome affects how you do your job or how your students learn, it's worth taking on right away. If it's more about your ego or a need to be right, consider talking it through once both parties have cooled down.

Finally, when you engage in conversation with a colleague with whom you disagree, try to use as many "I" statements as possible instead of "You" statements. For example, "I feel like we should take the students to the zoo on a field trip because it would bring the learning to life for our biology unit. I understand this would mean they miss soccer practice for Tuesday, but is there a way that the students would be able to still gain the skills they need to be able to play in the game?" (Compare this to a "You" statement such as, "You always put soccer first. Why can't you see that this field trip is more important than a soccer practice?")

Keep in mind

Usually, a conflict with a colleague can be solved with an honest face-to-face conversation, not a text or an email. Texts and emails can be forwarded, can be misinterpreted regarding tone, can lead to many gaps in understanding, and can sometimes feel attacking.

Tip #1

Focus on the problem at hand and finding a solution.

Tip #2

Be willing to compromise if this is a colleague you work closely with.

Tip #3

Listen to what they are saying and how they are feeling before you respond.

Tip #4

Use your compassionate voice to take control of the situation. Try to listen with an empathetic ear.

Tip #5

Have this conversation away from students and away from other colleagues, if possible.

Tip #6

Do not personally insult the colleague during the conversation. Focus on the specific issue at hand, not them personally. Failing to do so will only escalate the issue.

Tip #7

Be sure not to point fingers but, again, to focus on finding a solution.

Tip #8

For major conflicts, you might consider asking somebody you trust from administration to be a mediator during the conversation, but not to solve the issue for you. Use this tactic sparingly.

Tip #9

If you are having a conflict, think, *What's best for the students?* if that applies.

Tip #10

Think, *Could it be the colleague is just tired, stressed, or a bit on edge from being stretched too thin?*

Tip #11

If the conflict is purely about saving your ego, consider letting it go.

You may feel the impulse to . . .	Take a deep breath, and try this instead.
Take another teacher's behavior or words personally.	Consider that the other teacher might just be stressed or on edge from something completely unrelated to you. Give them the benefit of the doubt.
Ignore the conflict even after it happens a few times with the same colleague.	Ignore it if you can, but also remember that you deserve to feel valued and respected by colleagues in your workplace.
Form alliances to help you feel safe and secure emotionally at work.	Form healthy and positive friendships with colleagues.
Be condescending toward another teacher in front of students to "get back" at them.	Remember this is never appropriate. Every teacher deserves to be respected in front of students. Adult-to-adult conflict should be handled away from students—always.

Ask Yourself:

Is this conflict hurting my performance as a teacher, negatively affecting the students, or negatively affecting my own well-being? If yes, it's worth addressing.

Notes

AGENCY

How Can I Build a Supportive Relationship With Administrators?

You have the power to make your administration team your best allies or your worst enemies. As a teacher, your relationship with your administration will directly affect your job satisfaction. Let your students speak louder than you do. If you are doing an exciting project, the administration will hear about the excitement of the students! This will speak volumes for you.

If you are doing a display of learning, consider inviting administration in. Remember that their schedule is jam-packed; so if they do not show, don't take it personally. Consider having a student who often "gets in trouble" deliver the invitation if they have succeeded in this particular unit. This will strengthen your bond with that student as well as impress administration that you connected with the student on this particular project.

Sometimes you will need to ask directly for support from your administrators. Here are some examples of when asking for support may be necessary for maintaining your dynamic classroom:

- Mediating meetings with parents/caregivers that you anticipate will be difficult
- Handling extreme student behaviors or getting advice about how to handle behavior with students who may challenge you repeatedly (use sparingly)
- Sharing ideas or advice for instruction. Many administrators also have years of classroom experience.
- Providing constructive feedback to support your development as a teacher

Tip #1

Invite administrators to student presentations. Let them see your students at their best!

Tip #2

Attend school sporting or extracurricular events. Administration will notice, and so will your students.

Tip #3

Invite administrators to your room to participate in an engaging learning activity.

Tip #4

Give thank-you cards to administration at the end of every school year, listing something specific they did that helped you feel supported.

Tip #5

Show up to work consistently on time.

Tip #6

Speak about your students and colleagues respectfully. (Administration will hear your tone.)

You may feel the impulse to . . .	Take a deep breath, and try this instead.
Get frustrated that administration might not know about the great things you are doing in your classroom.	Remember that many times, administrators want to know about the great things going on in our classrooms but they might not get to hear about it from teachers. Let them know!
Get nervous that your students aren't silent when administration may stop by your room.	Remember that the administration doesn't necessarily want to see a silent room. Most likely, they want to see students engaged in what you are teaching. This may look different in different classrooms. Often, the most engaged classroom is the one where the teacher is hard to find when you first walk in because they are sitting in a group with students.
Think of teachers' relationship with administration as us versus them.	Know that administration is on your side. Even if they have not been educators before, they have the leadership skills to support you.

Ask Yourself:

How can I utilize the support of administration to benefit the learning in my classroom?

Notes

AGENCY

How Do I Work With a Co-teacher Effectively?

Access and Equity

Students should have access to both teachers and not always work with the same adult, no matter who the lead teacher technically is. Switch it up! One of the key components to co-teaching is reaching all learners.

You likely will have to work with another adult in your room and work with a co-teacher at some point in your career. This is when two or more teachers (usually only two) work together to teach a class or classes of different students. It's important that your students see the two of you as a united team. Having two adults in the classroom increases student access tremendously. Students have double the support to succeed in a lesson.

Recognize your co-teacher's strengths, and recognize them early. Is this person better at art? Better with technology? Better with attention to detail? Better with poetry? Better with public speaking? The beauty of co-teaching is that you both use your strengths to give the best to the students. This means knowing your own strengths as a teacher and how you both can complement each other. Have a growth mindset with each other. Is there something you can both learn from each other? Be open about this! You want to be stronger together as a united team than you would individually.

The students should be introduced to the two of you as a united team. This means placing both names on the door and both names on home communications. It's helpful to invest time getting to know your co-teacher in the beginning of the year and throughout. This may be the most important factor to your partnership working out with the students. This could look like eating lunch together once in a while, going to Starbucks, or going to a movie or even a yoga class together. Perhaps you can get together once a semester outside of school. No matter how much each of you knows about students or teaching, if you don't really get along personally and professionally, the students may be uncomfortable. It's awkward for the kids. Get to know your co-teacher as a human being as early as possible. This will help keep a positive classroom environment for both you and your students.

Tip #1

Rely on your co-teacher for something you might not be good at . . . yet.

Tip #2

Be willing to compromise, and be open to trying something new.

Tip #3

Clearly define your expectations for each other up front. How do you see each other working together? What does it look like on a day-to-day basis? On a weekly basis? Monthly?

Tip #4

Decide what mode of communication works for you. Do you not check email after a certain hour?

Do you take Sundays off? Do texts work better or emails? Is there an hour that is off limits to text after? Know that co-teaching takes a lot of communication. Set up what you are comfortable with up front.

Tip #5

Is there a small part of the lesson your co-teacher can take over daily so they are in front of the class at least once per lesson? Perhaps it's the vocab word for the day or the morning meeting.

Tip #6

Invite your co-teacher into the planning process so they can bring their ideas into the lesson. If you can have a weekly planning time you both honor, even better.

Tip #7

Praise your co-teacher when they do something well. It goes a long way.

Tip #8

Co-teachers can offer to help out with classroom "housekeeping" like grading and phone calls. This is an opportune time to use each other's strengths.

Keep in Mind

It's powerful when we view our co-teacher from an asset-based approach. So what experiences and knowledge does this teacher have that can benefit the classroom? What can they bring to the table that we might not be able to?

You may feel the impulse to . . .	Take a deep breath, and try this instead.
Argue or have a disagreement with your co-teacher about a student's behavior or an aspect of a lesson during class.	Remember that disagreeing in front of the students is counterproductive to creating a positive classroom environment. Talk about disagreements when students are not present.
Try to wing it with your co-teacher during the lesson.	Communicate with each other about the lesson prior to delivering it, or establish that the co-teacher always does the same part (e.g., co-teacher always does the word of the day or checks homework).
Have one of the adults revert to being the "disciplinarian" of the classroom.	Both adults are familiar with the classroom expectations and redirect students equally.
Vent to another teacher about how frustrated you are with your co-teacher.	This will eventually get back to your co-teacher and create an awkward relationship. It's best to vent to somebody outside of your work (if needed).
Hold in frustrations and avoid addressing them.	You both deserve to be happy in your workspace. Address frustrations with care and empathy.
Talk over each other in the lesson.	Let the teacher who is talking have the floor without interruption. Interrupting or correcting a co-teacher while they are teaching can undermine that adult in front of the class. If needed, pass a note to them or whisper to them.

AGENCY

Richard Villa and Jacqueline Thousand (2016) webinar, *Co-teaching to Increase Student Achievement*

https://www.youtube.com/watch?v=UrXqm6QunOY

It's important to mention that entire books have been written about co-teaching, and this topic cannot be thoroughly explored in just one section, yet a foundation of trust can be built based on this section. To learn more, access QR Code 5.1 for a webinar that takes an in-depth look at what co-teaching can look like in the classroom.

Ask Yourself:

What are my co-teacher's strengths, and how can they accentuate the lesson each day?

Notes

How Can I Creatively Get Parent and Caregiver Support From Day One?

> Many studies found that students with involved parents, no matter what their income or background, were more likely to earn higher grades and test scores, ... attend school regularly, have better social skills, show improved behavior, and adapt well to school.
>
> —ANNE T. HENDERSON AND KAREN L. MAPP,
> *A NEW WAVE OF EVIDENCE* (2002, P. 7)

A valuable lesson to help create your dynamic classroom is that parents and caregivers need to be and can be on your side. They do not need to be your best friends, but they can support you when needed. They can be a valuable resource. When a parent respects and admires you, their child will most likely follow suit. Parent support can look many different ways. It can be in the form of a parent understanding why a child doesn't do well on a test and working with the student at home to better understand the content. It can also look like a parent donating supplies to a classroom project or like a parent coming in to help you with a bulletin board or chaperone a field trip, to name just a few examples. Some parents will have more time to be involved than others, and it's important that we have empathy for parents in this sense. Keep in mind that just because a parent cannot come into the building in no way means they do not care.

Give opportunities for parents who speak English as a new language to also get involved. For example, when planning a project presentation, although the projects might be in English, a bilingual student in your classroom may be able to translate your welcoming introduction to parents before you begin the presentation. This is also strong public speaking practice for that student. Give that student translator a copy of what you will be saying a few days ahead, and let them translate. Two students can also do this together.

You can't go wrong reaching out to parents. You may want to explain to the class the day before why the parent is coming in so the students can interact with your guest. You could say something like this as an introduction and to review expectations:

"Tomorrow, class, I have invited Mrs. Smith, a parent volunteer, in to (purpose of visit). I would not invite a parent into every class, but I trust this class is mature enough to have a guest. It is important that you say good morning to Mrs. Smith and understand she is dedicating her own free time to help our learning. Make sure you also thank Mrs. Smith for the time she is giving our classroom."

How Can I Creatively Get Parent and Caregiver Support From Day One?

121

✳ ⌐ Tip #1 ⌐

Send a postcard home during the summer, introducing yourself and saying how excited you are to be their child's teacher, to connect to that parent from the start. (This shows you are on top of it!)

✳ ⌐ Tip #2 ⌐

Have students make parent invitations to deliver to their parents or guardians when you have projects to show or presentations. Parents love being audience members and coming to presentations.

✳ ⌐ Tip #3 ⌐

Invite parents to come in for read-alouds (depending on the grade). Students can increase their reading level and comprehension by reading to parents, or parents can read to students, depending on your goal.

✳ ⌐ Tip #4 ⌐

Invite parents to come in to help with themed bulletin boards. Have them write inspirational messages on the boards.

✳ ⌐ Tip #5 ⌐

Ask parents to be classroom volunteers you can call on when needed throughout the school year.

✳ ⌐ Tip #6 ⌐

Get a stamp that requests parent signatures. Add an extra point to the scores of students who bring back the assignment with a parent signature. Parents love to know what assignments their child is completing.

✳ ⌐ Tip #7 ⌐

Have parent guest speakers if they can speak directly to your unit of study. For example, invite a scientist if you are teaching a chemistry class, a nurse if you are teaching about biology, or a judge if you are reading *To Kill a Mockingbird*.

✳ ⌐ Tip #8 ⌐

Invite parents to come in on editing day for major pieces of writing or poetry (especially fiction or creative writing). Parents will love to give input to students about their writing—and the more eyes the better.

✳ ⌐ Tip #9 ⌐

Invite parents to chaperone field trips.

Tip #10

Have a classroom career fair with parents or relatives of students. Each parent can have a table and talk about what they do every day, and students can rotate around them.

Tip #11

Invite parents to come in to lead a learning station. Invite a parent to come read to the class as a whole. The students will appreciate the new voice in the room.

Tip #12

Have a parent mixer or barbeque for your classroom at the beginning of the school year. When parents are friends, your job can become easier. For instance, two parents who are friends can support you on a field trip, help with read-alouds, or help with a bulletin board.

Great Resources

- Blog post: Boult, B. (2016, June 29). 10 tips for engaging parents. *Corwin Connect.* https://corwin-connect.com/2016/06/10-tips-engaging-parents/

- Book: Boult, B. (2016). *201 ways to involve parents* (3rd ed.). Corwin.

- Book: Kreisberg, H., & Beyranevand, M. L. (2021). *Partnering with parents in elementary school math.* Corwin.

You may feel the impulse to . . .	Take a deep breath, and try this instead.
Get frustrated if some parents do not want to be involved.	Remember it is a parent's choice to be involved or not, but they will never be angry to have at least been invited in.
Not involve parents for fear that they'll make your job harder.	Think of a few parents who could make your job easier and maximize the learning of the classroom.

Ask Yourself:

How could parent engagement make your classroom more dynamic? What are some ways parents could help?

Notes

AGENCY

How Do I Build Healthy Parent and Caregiver Relationships?

Equity and Access

Assume parents are doing their best. You may want to consider sending a questionnaire home in the beginning of the year, asking parents for the best times and methods for communicating. You may have to get creative, too!

Parents and caregivers can be a valuable resource. When a parent respects and admires you, most likely the child will do the same. And unfortunately, if a parent feels the opposite, more often than not, the child will also feel the same. It's beneficial if parents know you a bit so everything they hear is not through the lens of their child. Even if the child does support you, there will be days when they may not, because students, like us, have good days and bad days. This is why building healthy, supportive relationships with parents and caregivers is crucial. Remember that *parents and caregivers are doing what they think is best for their child based on what they know.* Parents and caregivers act out of love and concern. If you understand this, you can empathize with them.

In the beginning of the year, have students share some personal interests, hobbies, or skills in an icebreaker or on a note card. This way, when you meet with a parent you can talk about the interests of their child in conversation. This shows you genuinely care about the whole child, not just the academic side. Parents will warm up to you a bit if you know their child on a personal level.

Remember that parents may have different forms of routines and structures in their houses and it's important we do not judge. Every household has different routines and amounts of structure. This may make it more difficult for some students to find a quiet place to read or study.

Also, the student may have two working parents or a single parent working multiple jobs to make ends meet. It is important that, as teachers, we do not mistake these parents as "not caring" because they are not as present at school functions or meetings.

In many classrooms, there will be parents who do not speak or read English fluently. These parents may not have access to the information you are sending home and may, in turn, shy away from being involved in the classroom or in their child's education. If you have access to Google Translate, it will be helpful to translate important information into other languages. You could do one side in English and the other side in another language. Or it may be helpful to gently remind parents to set up a translator relative, neighbor, or other adult who can help them stay in the loop with parent classroom communication if needed. Ask your administration, too, what translation or interpreter services are available through the school or district.

Tip #1

Communicate early and often.

Tip #2

Make positive phone calls home, especially for students who may not always do so well in school.

Create a monthly newsletter for parents.

Introduce yourself at the beginning of the year.

The first communication with a parent should be positive! You do not want your first interaction to be about behavior or academic issues.

Educate yourself about community programs available for families. This way you can share these programs with parents in meetings if needed. Counselors are a great resource to help find these programs.

Be able to defend a child's grade with examples of work.

Offer support to their child through tutoring, office hours, and school programs.

Talk about and know at least one of a student's strengths when communicating with their parent or guardian.

You may feel the impulse to . . .	Take a deep breath, and try this instead.
Contact parents only when students are misbehaving.	Contact parents early in the school year, first with a quick hello/email/postcard.
Respond to every parent email and correspondence immediately.	Give yourself 72 hours to respond. Your first job is to teach students.
Hope parents respect your boundaries with contact times and correspondence.	Be clear (but gentle) with your wording about "business hours" in a parent letter or email in the beginning of the year.

Ask Yourself:

How can I communicate with parents often and efficiently?

Notes

AGENCY

How Do I Navigate a Difficult Meeting With a Parent or Caregiver?

Keep in Mind

A difficult meeting is not the first time a parent or caregiver should hear from the teacher all school year. That is why it is important to reach out to parents early in the school year to build a foundational relationship *before* you need their support.

Teachers all have meetings with parents about difficult topics or have to meet with parents who don't see things the way we do. Chances are you will have to defend a decision about a student grade or other issue at some point in the school year. You may have to rectify a situation. Difficult meetings are where our true professionalism and strength of character come out. They are where our words can be daggers or saviors, where we might see tears and laughs. Through practice, teachers can get better at compassionately handling difficult meetings.

When we have difficult meetings, it's important that as teachers we come to the meeting understanding that this parent is trying their best, just as we are. A difficult parent meeting can be hard for a parent because they often feel like their child is a reflection of them. They may feel judged or embarrassed. It's important that we let the parents know we are on the same team, all supporting the child. It's important to remember that this parent or caregiver saw this child's first steps and heard their first words. Be gentle yet firm with your wording and tone. You want this parent on your side to support the student by the end of the meeting.

Agency and Identity

In almost all circumstances, students can and should be invited into the meeting as well. This empowers students to be a part of the conversation and usually makes the meeting more powerful and effective.

How to Navigate a Difficult Meeting With a Parent or Caregiver

1. Shake hands with the parent and student. (It's a really good idea to invite the student in, too, so everybody is on the same page.)

2. Empower the student and let them talk. Do not interrupt; just listen. If they say something that is accusatory or just not accurate, respond

with, "I'm sorry you feel that way." (Be careful not to be condescending in your tone here. Be genuine.)

3. Then start your part with a student strength: "Sarah, I really value having you in class because you always raise your hand and have something to say, even when the others may not participate as much." It's important to have one strength ready to go before the meeting.

4. Then transition to something like, "However, sometimes you use that strength at inappropriate times. There have been times when we had to complete assignments and you were talking with a friend. This caused a lower grade. Would you agree with that statement?" Most will agree here.

5. Ask, "What can I do to help you talk less during independent work time?"

6. The student will either shrug their shoulders or ask you to move their seat at this point. Most likely, the parent will jump in and ask that you contact home if this happens again.

7. You can suggest a plan of action to help the student succeed and explain your decision to the student and parent so everybody is on the same page.

8. Give the student a sticky note with three action items they are to work on. Have the student keep it in their binder to empower them to make the change.

9. Make sure before you leave you have the most up-to-date contact (other emails, phone numbers, etc.) for the parent.

10. You most likely now have that parent's support.

Equity and Access

In meetings where parents of students do not speak English, schools can provide translators (ask your administration for your school's policy or support system for this). Or perhaps ask a colleague to assist.

You may feel the impulse to . . .	Take a deep breath, and try this instead.
Take a difficult parent meeting personally.	Remember that this parent is doing what they think is best for their child.
Not prepare for your meeting because you're too busy or too irritated.	Have strong documentation (dates, assignments, etc.) to compassionately back up your meeting.
Just give up on a student because the parents are unreachable.	Remember that these are the students who need you the most. Hang in there.

Ask Yourself:

• Did this student leave feeling empowered and knowing how to improve in class?
• Does the parent or guardian feel like we are on the same team to support this student?

Notes

AGENCY

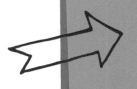

How Do I Pick Myself Back Up After I Mess Up?

> Every day's a new day. Always give your students the opportunity to make good choices. Be flexible; things happen, so go with the flow. Smile and show students that you care; you may be the only person who does. Also, be calm and patient.
>
> —MS. SAFT, EARLY CHILDHOOD ELEMENTARY SCHOOL TEACHER

Teaching is an on-the-feet sort of job. You are constantly making split-second decisions and dealing with hundreds of people on a daily basis. It's not a sit-in-your-office-and-close-the-door kind of job, and that's the beauty of it. We're rarely alone. Not to mention that we are basically giving performances in front of people every single day. Mistakes will happen, and that's okay.

Teaching is all about picking ourselves back up after we mess up. Even the most experienced teachers mess up sometimes, but they have learned to recover with ease and learn from their mistakes. The way we get better and stronger as teachers is in how we think about our "mess-ups" and how we get better tomorrow from our mistakes today. When we make a mistake, it's important to take time and reflect on what we could have done differently, reflect on what we learned from the mistake and get better tomorrow. Think of every mess-up as a growth opportunity, not a reason to get weaker. It can be helpful for students to see an adult work through a mistake and learn from it. This is modeling how to keep a growth mindset in your dynamic classroom.

Tip #1

Journal about what's on your mind to reflect and problem-solve.

Tip #2

Talk to a trusted colleague to get it off your chest—and to ask for suggestions or help, if necessary.

Tip #3

Try some deep breathing, and imagine yourself exhaling any negative feelings about the mistake you made.

Tip #4

Apologize earnestly, if it's in order, and always take responsibility.

You may feel the impulse to . . .	Take a deep breath, and try this instead.
Give in to feelings of embarrassment, shame, or sadness after you mess up.	Remember that mistakes are a part of growth. If you aren't making mistakes, you aren't growing. It's all about how you pick yourself back up. The best teachers do this well.
Ruminate on what went wrong, replaying it in your head over and over again.	Give yourself permission to think about it for a bit if needed, then think about or discuss with a co-teacher what could have been done differently.
Not try an activity again if the students' behavior was substandard the first time you tried it.	Don't be afraid to try it again sometime! But before you do, lead a class reflection of what worked well and what could be better next time. Make a class chart based on student input. Revisit this chart after the activity, and praise them for the growth. Keep doing this.
Worry the students will hold a grudge if you mess up a lesson.	Know that students are extremely forgiving and often forget about mess-ups. They are usually more forgiving than adults.

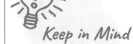

Keep in Mind

It's important not to ruminate on something if you mess up. Pick yourself back up, and move on. Don't let striving to be perfect get in the way of being good at something.

Ask Yourself:

Am I using the times I've messed up as learning opportunities to help me grow as a teacher?

Notes

_____

_____

_____

_____

_____

_____

_____

_____

_____

_____

_____

_____

_____

AGENCY

What Small Tweaks Make a Profound Difference in My Job Satisfaction and Overall Well-Being?

> Do everything you can in the beginning of the year to create a sense of community within your classroom. This takes time at first but goes a long way when your students feel ownership of the room and group!
>
> —MELISSA PARISER, FORMER ELEMENTARY SCHOOL TEACHER AND COUNSELOR

There are small things you can do to make a huge difference in your job satisfaction and how much you enjoy being at work every day. This section will list just a few that seem to have the most impact on satisfied teachers.

Tip #1

Be mindful about who you surround yourself with at work. *It's been said you are the average of the five people you spend the most time with. So purposefully spend the most time with teachers you admire and respect.*

Tip #2

In the beginning of the year, integrate get-to-know-you activities and other activities that bond the class together. *Your goal is to create a community of learners. These fun activities also help you get to know the students on a personal level, which will help them feel more connected to you as a teacher.*

Tip #3

At lunch or during your prep, carve out five to ten minutes (or more if you can) to take a walk around the school. Get your heart pumping. Be proactive and avoid walking where you know there might be distractions. *A quick walk around school gets you outside and the blood flowing, which is vital to good mental health and stamina.*

Tip #4

When stressors interrupt your day, take a break and do something else. Snap your mind out of fixating on the negativity. *When you change what you are doing, your mind can break out of a negative pattern or stop ruminating on something.*

Tip #5

Consider getting into a routine of meal prepping for the week to eat healthy, keep yourself energized, and feel your best. *Starbucks can only do so much and isn't* as sustainable as healthy eating habits. Healthy eating habits increase mental performance, increase energy, and help with eliminating mood swings.

Tip #6

Consider keeping healthy snacks and water in your room as well. *You may get hungry throughout the day, when you still have a long way to go before lunch and three more classes to teach. Very few teachers can teach well on an empty stomach. A quick granola bar can do wonders.*

Tip #7

Know when it's time to unplug—and then do that without guilt. *There will always be one more thing to do, and sometimes we just need a break.*

Tip #8

Keep a drawer for student or colleague thank-you notes. If you are having a rough day, open that drawer and enjoy. *It's easy to forget the good when things aren't going your way.*

You may feel the impulse to . . .	Take a deep breath, and try this instead.
Vent to toxic colleagues because it's easy.	Find healthier ways to connect with colleagues.
Feel like a victim when the school year gets tough.	Take control of your workload and tasks small steps at a time. It adds up.
Forgo healthy eating for lack of time and resort to fast food or unhealthy meals.	Healthy eating is even more important for teachers, who are expected to take care of so many people and have limited time throughout the day.

Ask Yourself:

What small steps can I start doing today that can make a profound difference in my overall well-being as a teacher?

Notes

AGENCY

What Are Some Effective Time-Saving Hacks?

We all wish we had more time. The good news is that there are strategies that can help you feel like you have more time in the school day. Effective time management will improve your confidence and morale, energize and engage your students, and add to the positive and organized climate of your classroom.

Strong time management skills make for a healthy learning environment for both you and the students. Students deserve teachers who are energized, optimistic, and in control of the daily grind while still having energy and time to foster meaningful connections. Develop proactive habits for managing time, and give your best self to your students.

It's important to remember to be mindful with how you talk about your time, too. Words have power. Habits have just as much power, if not more. How you spend your time at work is probably similar day to day. Doing a time audit for one full day every so often can help you bring to light what you value and what you spend the most and least time on. A time audit will give you a clear perspective on what you are spending too much or too little time on.

Tip #1

Don't grade everything. Grade assignments that prove mastery of what you are teaching. Offering consistent feedback will be more helpful to students and will save you grading time in the long run.

Tip #2

Make copies a few days (or a week, optimally) in advance to save time and frustration when there is a long line or when the copier breaks down temporarily (and it will).

Tip #3

Pass out papers before the lesson, and refer to them as you are teaching. If students are in groups, place groups of papers facedown in the center of the desks so students can quickly refer to them as they need in a lesson.

Tip #4

Trying to do everything at once actually takes more time. Make a list of what you need to do, prioritize, and do each task from start to finish.

Tip #5

Make a list of what you need to do during your prep to efficiently use your time.

Tip #6

Listen to music to keep focus during your prep, before school, or after school. Music can keep your mind from wandering as you are doing jobs around your classroom.

Tip #7

Set up for the next day before you leave your classroom every afternoon. This not only saves you time in the morning but gives you peace of mind that evening to recharge.

Tip #8

Use a timer to get started on dreaded tasks that you can't seem to face. Set the timer for 10 minutes, and start the task. You can stop when the 10 minutes are finished, but you'll probably find you'll want to go longer because you have gained momentum.

Tip #9

Delegate some tasks to students. This not only saves you time but gives students a sense of belonging in your classroom.

Keep in Mind

Beware of "shiny object syndrome," when you are distracted by every new thing that comes your way. This leads to wasting valuable time.

You may feel the impulse to . . .	Take a deep breath, and try this instead.
Try to do everything at once.	Know that multitasking actually isn't possible. Make a list of what you need to do, in order of importance, and do each of those tasks from start to finish.
Spend time ruminating on problems.	Focus on what you can do right now. Ruminating on problems or allowing negativity into your mind and body can be a thief of time and energy.

Ask Yourself:

Is there something I've been spending too much time on? How can I adjust this?

Notes

AGENCY

Recap: Try This Tomorrow

Each of these strategies takes little prep and can help you uncover the answers to issues we often don't initially talk about but need to know how to address.

- Schedule self-care into your calendar as you would any meeting or work obligation.
- Take action on stressors you can control.
- Be willing to have hard conversations with colleagues if necessary, if they are worth having.
- Speak about your students respectfully. (Administration will hear your tone.)
- After a parent meeting, give the student or parent (preferably the student) a sticky note with three action items they are to work on (assignments to raise grades, etc.). Have the student keep it in their binder to empower them to make the change.
- Praise your co-teacher for something they did well, no matter how big or small.
- Consider getting into a routine of meal prepping for the week to eat healthy and keep yourself energized and feeling your best.
- Talk about your self-care with colleagues. When you talk about it, you are telling others it is important to you, and perhaps someone will join you.
- Don't grade everything. Grade only assignments that prove mastery of what you are teaching.
- Have students make parent invitations to deliver to their parents or guardians when you have projects to show or presentations. Parents love being audience members.
- If you need to have a difficult meeting with a parent about student behavior or grades, ask the parent to bring the student as well. You should all be on the same page.

Notes

Answers to Your Biggest Questions About Creating a Dynamic Classroom

REFERENCES

Abrams, J. (2016). *Hard conversations unpacked.* Corwin.

Berger, R. (2012, March 9). *Austin's butterfly: Building excellence in student work* [Video]. Vimeo. https://vimeo.com/38247060

Berkeley Center for Teaching & Learning. (n.d.). *Rubrics.* https://teaching.berkeley.edu/resources/improve/evaluate-course-level-learning/rubrics

Brock, B., & Grady, M. (2002). *Avoiding burnout: A principal's guide to keeping the fire alive.* Corwin.

Camera, L. (2021, July 27). Study confirms school-to-prison pipeline. *US News & World Report.* https://www.usnews.com/news/education-news/articles/2021–07-27/study-confirms-school-to-prison-pipeline

Centre for Teaching Excellence, University of Waterloo. (n.d.). *Implementing group work in the classroom.* https://uwaterloo.ca/centre-for-teaching-excellence/teaching-resources/teaching-tips/alternatives-lecturing/group-work/implementing-group-work-classroom

Delpit, L. (2013). *Multiplication is for white people.* New Press.

Dweck, C. (2016). *Mindset: The new psychology of success* (updated ed.). Ballantine Books.

Edutopia. (2021, July 14). *Education buzz words defined: What is differentiation?* [Video]. YouTube. https://www.youtube.com/watch?v=GkZUXdT0WcY

Fisher, D., Frey, N., Bustamante, V., & Hattie, J. (2020). *The assessment playbook for distance and blended learning.* Corwin.

Gage, N. L., & Berliner, D. C. (1992). *Educational psychology* (5th ed.). Houghton Mifflin.

Garcia, A. (2021, June 17). Words matter: The case for shifting to "emergent bilingual." *Language Magazine.* https://www.languagemagazine.com/2021/06/17/words-matter-the-case-for-shifting-to-emergent-bilingual/

Goldberg, M. (2021, June 28). Feeling burned out? These expert-approved strategies will help you recover. *Oprah Daily.* https://www.oprahdaily.com/life/a36801181/how-to-recover-from-burnout/

Gonzalez, V. (2020, September 22). What is the affective filter, and why is it important in the classroom? *Seidlitz Education.* https://seidlitzblog.org/2020/09/22/what-is-the-affective-filter-and-why-is-it-important-in-the-classroom/

Harris, A. (2021, July 2). A better way to check student understanding. *Corwin Connect.* https://corwin-connect.com/2021/07/a-better-way-to-check-student-understanding/

Hattie, J. (2012). *Visible learning for teachers: Maximizing impact on learning.* Routledge.

Hattie, J. (2018, October). 250+ influences on student achievement. *Corwin Visible Learning.* https://us.corwin.com/sites/default/files/250_influences_10.1.2018.pdf

Henderson, A. T., & Mapp, K. L. (2002). *A new wave of evidence: The impact of school, family, and community connections on student achievement.* National Center for Family and Community Connections with Schools, Southwest Educational Development Laboratory.

Karpinski, E. (2021). *Put happiness to work.* McGraw Hill.

Marzano, R. J., Marzano, J. S., & Pickering, D. J. (2003). *Classroom management that works.* ASCD.

Pariser, S. (2018). *Real talk about classroom management.* Corwin.

Pariser, S., & DeRoche, E. (2020). *Real talk about time management.* Corwin.

Schawbel, D. (2018, November 13). Why work friendships are critical for long-term happiness. *CNBC: At Work.* https://www.cnbc.com/2018/11/13/why-work-friendships-are-critical-for-long-term-happiness.html

Simona. (2021, March 31). The 5 stages of burnout. *Vitrue VIDA.* https://vitrueremote.com/5-stages-of-burnout/

Snyder, S., & Fenner, D. (2021). *Culturally responsive teaching for multilingual learners.* Corwin.

TeachThought Staff. (n.d.). *How many decisions do teachers make in a day?* TeachThought. https://www.teachthought.com/pedagogy/teacher-makes-1500-decisions-a-day/

Thousand, J. S., Villa, R. A., & Nevin, A. I. (2015). *Differentiating instruction: Planning for universal* design and teaching for college and career readiness (2nd ed.). Corwin.

Tucker, C. (2017, December 28). Rethink your grading practices. *Dr. Catlin Tucker.* https://catlintucker.com/2017/12/grading-practices/

Tucker, C. R., Wycoff, T., & Green, J. T. (2017). *Blended learning in action.* Corwin.

Villa, R., & Thousand, J. (2016, October 19). *Co-teaching to increase student achievement* [Video]. https://www.youtube.com/watch?v=UrXqm6Qun0Y

Watson, A. (2014, January 20). 50 fun call and response ideas to get students' attention. *Angela Watson's Truth for Teachers.* https://truthforteachers.com/50-fun-call-and-response-ideas-to-get-students-attention/

What are the 5 stages of burnout? (2020, August 20). Calmer. https://www.thisiscalmer.com/blog/5-stages-of-burnout

Wigert, B. (2020, March 13). Employee burnout: The biggest myth. *Gallup.* https://www.gallup.com/workplace/288539/employee-burnout-biggest-myth.aspx

Wolpert-Gawron, H. (2018). *Just ask us: Kids speak out on student engagement.* Corwin.

Wong, H. K., & Wong, R. T. (2009). *The first days of school: How to be an effective teacher.* Harry K. Wong Publications.

INDEX

Confident Teachers, Inspired Learners

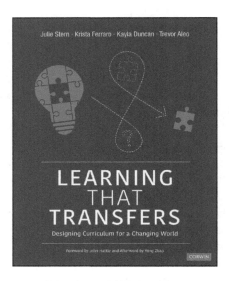

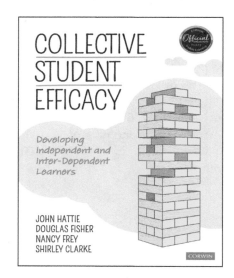

No matter where you are in your professional journey, Corwin aims to ease the many demands teachers face on a daily basis with accessible strategies that benefit ALL learners.

CAROL PELLETIER RADFORD

Equip teachers with the tools they need to take care of themselves so they can serve their students, step into leadership, and contribute to the education profession.

STEPAN MEKHITARIAN

Combine the best of distance learning and classroom instruction with a new vision for learning and professional development that capitalizes on the distance learning experience.

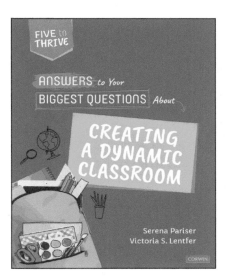

SERENA PARISER, VICTORIA S. LENTFER

Find actionable answers to your most pressing questions on how to create and sustain dynamic classroom.

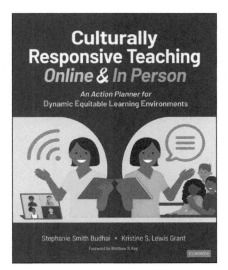

STEPHANIE SMITH BUDHAI, KRISTINE S. LEWIS GRANT

Help teachers pivot instruction to ensure equitable, inclusive learning experiences in online and in-person settings.

A SAGE Publishing Company

Helping educators make the greatest impact

CORWIN HAS ONE   MISSION: to enhance education through intentional professional learning.

We build long-term relationships with our authors, educators, clients, and associations who partner with us to develop and continuously improve the best evidence-based practices that establish and support lifelong learning.